The Story of Early Ohio

Indians, Frontiersmen, Pioneers, Statesmen and Wars

Re-created from the book "*Stories of Ohio*" by

William Dean Howells

Originally published in 1897

with

Additional and Enhanced Illustrations, Addendums and Annotations

added by

C. Stephen Badgley

2014

ISBN 978-0615988184

This book is part of the Historical Collection of Badgley Publishing Company and has been re-created from the original book "*Stories of Ohio*" by William Dean Howells and published in 1897. The original contents have been edited and corrections have been made to original printing, spelling and grammatical errors when not in conflict with the author's intent to portray a particular event or interaction. Annotations have been made and additional content has been added by Badgley Publishing Company in order to clarify certain historical events or interactions and to enhance the author's content. Photos and illustrations from the original have been touched up, enhanced and sometimes enlarged for better viewing. Additional illustrations and photos have been added by Badgley Publishing Company.

THE STORY OF EARLY OHIO

Preface

(From the original book *"Stories of Ohio" Published* in 1897)

In the following stories, drawn from the annals of Ohio, I have tried to possess the reader with knowledge, in outline at least, of the history of the State from the earliest times. I cannot suppose that I have done this with unfailing accuracy in respect to fact, but with regard to the truth, I am quite sure of my purpose at all times to impart it.

The books which have been of most use to me in writing this are the histories of Francis Parkman; the various publications of Messrs. Robert Clarke and Co. in the *"Ohio Valley Series"*; McClung's *"Sketches of Western Adventure"*; *"Ohio"* (in the American Commonwealths Series) by Rufus King; *"History and Civil Government of Ohio"* by B. A. Hinsdale and Mary Hinsdale; *"Beginnings of Literary Culture in the Ohio Valley"* by W. H. Venable; Theodore Roosevelt's *"Winning of the West"*; Whitelaw Reid's *"Ohio in the War"*; and above all others, the delightful and inexhaustible volumes of Henry Howe's *"Historical Collections of Ohio."*

William Dean Howells
1897

William Dean Howells
1837 - 1920

Chapter One

The Ice Folk and the Earth Folk

THE first Ohio stories are part of the common story of the wonderful Ice Age, when a frozen deluge pushed down from the north and covered a vast part of the earth's surface with slowly moving glaciers. The traces that this age left in Ohio are much the same as it left elsewhere and the signs that there were people here ten thousand years ago, when the glaciers began to melt and the land became fit to live in again, are such as have been found in the glacier drift in many other countries. Even before the ice came creeping southwestwardly from the region of Niagara, and passed over two thirds of our state, from Lake Erie to the Ohio River, there were people here of a race older than the hills, as the hills now are. For the glaciers ground away the hills as they once were and made new ones, with new valleys between them and new channels for the streams to run where there had never been water courses before.

These earliest Ohioans must have been the same as the Ohioans of the Ice Age and when they had fled southward before the glaciers, they must have followed the retreat of the melting ice back into Ohio again. No one knows how long they dwelt here along its edges in a climate like that of Greenland, where the glaciers are now to be seen as they once were in the region of Cincinnati. But it is believed that these Ice Folk, as we may call them, were of the race which still roams the Arctic snows. They seem to have lived as the Eskimos of our day live; they were hunters and fishers, and in the gravelly banks of the new rivers, which the glaciers upheaved, the Ice Folk dropped the axes of chipped stone which are now found there. They left nothing else behind them; but similar tools or weapons are found in the glacier-built river banks of Europe, and so it is thought that the race of the earliest Ohio men lived pretty much all over the world in the Ice Age. One of the learned writers, Professor G. F. Wright, who is surest of them and has told us most about them, holds that they were for their time and place as worthy ancestors as any people could have; and we could well believe this because the Ohio man has, in all ages, been one of the foremost men.

Our Ice Folk were sturdy, valiant, and cunning enough to cope with the fierce brute life and the terrible climate of their day, but all they have left to prove it is the same kind of stone axes that have been found in the rift of the glaciers, along the water courses in Northern France and Southern England.

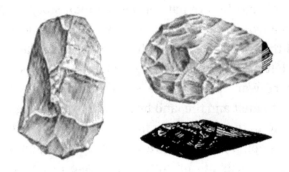

Our Ice Folk must have dressed like their far descended children, the Eskimos, in furs and skins, and like them they must have lived upon fish and the flesh of wild beasts. The least terrible of these beasts would have been the white bear; the mammoth and mastodon were among the animals the Ice Folk hunted for game, and slew them without bows or arrows, for there was no wood to make these. The only weapon the Ice Folk had was the stone ax which they may have struck into their huge prey when they came upon it sleeping or followed in the chase till it dropped with fatigue. Such an ax was dug up out of the glacial terrace, as the bank of this drift is called, in the valley of the Tuscarawas, in 1889, perhaps ten thousand years after it was left there. It was wrought from a piece of black flint, four inches long and two inches wide. At the larger end it was nearly as thick as it was wide, and it was chipped to a sharp edge all round. Within the present year another of the Ice Folk's axes has been found near New London, twenty-two feet underground, in the same kind of glacial drift as the first. But it seems to have been made of a different kind of stone and to have been so deeply rotted by the long ages it had been buried that when its outer substance was scratched away, hardly anything of the hard green rock was left.

After the glaciers were gone, the Ohio climate was still very cold, and vast lakes stretched over the state, freezing in the long winters and thawing in the short summers. One of these spread upward from the neighborhood of Akron to the east and west of where Cleveland stands. But by far, the largest flooded nearly all that part of Ohio which the glaciers failed to cover, from beyond where Pittsburg is to where

Cincinnati is. At the last point a mighty ice dam formed every winter till, as the climate grew warmer and the ice thawed more and more, the waters burst the dam and poured their tide down the Ohio River to the Mississippi while those of the northern lake rushed through the Cuyahoga to Lake Erie and both lakes disappeared forever.

For the next four or five thousand years the early Ohio men kept very quiet; but we need not suppose for that reason that there were none. Our Ice Folk, who dropped their stone axes in the river banks, may have passed away with the Ice Age or they may have remained in Ohio and begun slowly to take on some faint likeness of civilization. There is nothing to prove that they went and there is nothing to prove that they stayed, but Ohio must always have been a pleasant place to live after the great thaw and it seems reasonable to think that the Ice Folk lingered, in part at least, and changed with the changing climate and became at last a people who left the signs of their presence in almost every part of the state.

These were the Mound Builders, whose works are said to be two or three thousand years old, though we cannot be very sure of that. There are some who think that the mounds are only a few hundred years old and that their builders were the race of red men whom the white men found here. One may think very much as one likes, and I like to think that the Mound Builders were a very ancient people who vanished many ages before the Indians came here. They could not have been savages, for the region where they dwelt could not have fed savages enough to heap up the multitude of their mounds. Each wild man needs fifty thousand acres to live upon, as the wild man lives by hunting and fishing. In the whole Ohio country, the earliest white adventurers found only two or three thousand Indians at the most and the people who built those forts and temples and tombs, and shaped from the earth the mighty images of their strange bird-gods and reptile-gods, could have lived only by tilling the soil. Their mounds are found everywhere in the west between the Alleghany Mountains and the Mississippi River, but they are found mostly in Ohio where their farms and gardens once bordered the Muskingum, the Scioto, the two Miamis and our other large streams, which they probably used as highways to the rivers of the southwest.

Their forts were earthworks, but they were skillfully planned, with a knowledge which no savage race has shown. They were real strongholds and they are so large that some of them enclose hundreds of acres within walls of earth which still rise ten and twelve feet from the ground. They are on a far grander scale than the supposed temples or religious works and there are more of them than of all the other ruins, except the small detached mounds, which are almost numberless.

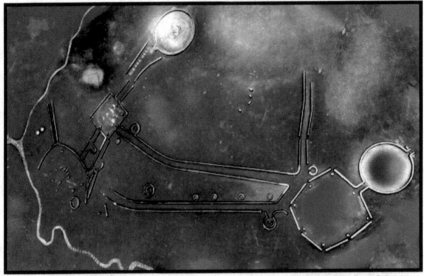

Layout of the ancient earthworks at present day Newark, Ohio

Layout of the ancient earthworks at present day Marietta, Ohio

These, from the charred bones found among the ashes in them, are known to be tombs and they were probably the sepulchers of the common people whose bodies were burned. The large mounds are heaped above walled chambers and in these were platforms, supposed to have been altars, and whole skeletons, supposed to be the skeletons of priests buried there. The priests are supposed to have been the chiefs of the people and to have ruled them through their superstitions. But there is nothing to prove this, for their laws were never put in written words or any other sign of speech. In some of the mounds little figures of burnt clay have been found which may be idols, and pieces of ancient pottery, which may be fragments of sacred vessels, and small plates of copper, with marks or scratches on them, which may be letters. Some antiquarians have tried to read these letters, if they are letters, and to make sense out of them, but no seeker after true Ohio stories can trust their interpretations.

This skeleton was found in a mound in Adams County, Ohio without lower legs. If whole, it would have measured between 7 and 8 feet tall.

The Mound Builders used very little stone and showed no knowledge of masonry. But they built so massively out of the earth that their works have lasted to this day in many places, just as they left them, except for the heavy growth of trees which the first settlers found covering them and which were sometimes seven or eight hundred years old. At Marietta, these works, when the white people came, were quite perfect and enclosed fifty acres on the bank of the Muskingum overlooking the

Ohio. They were in great variety of design. The largest mound was included in the grounds of the present cemetery and so has been saved, but the plow of the New England emigrant soon passed over the foundations of the Mound Builders' temples.

At Circleville the shape of their fortifications gave its name to the town, which has long since hid them from sight. One of them was almost perfectly round and the other nearly square. The round fort was about seventy feet in diameter and was formed of two walls twenty feet high, with a deep ditch between. The other fort was fifty-five rods square and it had no ditch. Seven gateways opened into it at the side and corners and it was joined to the round fort by an eighth.

It is forever to be regretted that these precious ancient works should have been destroyed to make place for the present town, but within a few years one of the most marvelous of the Mound Builders' works, the great Serpent Mound near Loudon, in Adams County has been preserved to after time by the friends of science and put in the keeping of the Peabody Museum at Harvard University. The state of Ohio has passed a law protecting the land around it as a park and there is now reason to hope that the mound will last as long as the rocky bluff on which the serpent lies coiled. This huge idol is more than twelve hundred feet long and is the most wonderful symbol in the world of the serpent worship, which was everywhere, the earliest religion of our race.

The largest military ruin is the famous Fort Ancient in Warren County, where, on a terrace above the Little Miami River, five miles of wall, which can still be easily traced, shut in a hundred acres. In Highland County, about seventeen miles southeast of Hillsborough, another great fortress embraces thirty-five acres on the crest of a hill overlooking

Brush Creek. Its walls are some twenty-five feet wide at the base and rise from six to ten feet above the ground. Within their circuit are two ponds which could supply water in time of siege and in the valley, which the hill commands, are the ruins of the Mound Builders' village whose people could take refuge in the fort on the hilltop and hold it against any approaching force.

Fort Ancient Earthworks
What they may have looked like almost 2000 years ago.

For the rest, the works of the Mound Builders, except such as were too large to be destroyed by the farmer, have disappeared almost as wholly as the Mound Builders themselves. Their mole-like race threw up their ridges and banks and larger and lesser heaps and then ceased from the face of the earth, as utterly as if they had burrowed into its heart. They may have fled before the ancestors of the savages whom our ancestors found here, they may have passed down peacefully into Mexico and built the cities which the Spaniards destroyed there. Or, they may have come up out of Mexico and lost the higher arts of their civilization in our northern woods, warring with the wild tribes who were here before them. In either case, it is imaginable that the Mound Builders were of the same race as the ancient Mexicans and Peruvians, and it is probable that they were akin to the Zunis of our own day. The snake dances of the Zunis are a relic of the old serpent worship and the fear and hate which the Zunis bear the red savages of the plains may be another heritage from the kindred race which once peopled our Ohio valleys.

Chapter Two
Ohio as a Part of France

IF the people of Ohio were Eskimos in the ages before history began, and then thousands of years after, but still thousands of years ago were Aztecs, there is no doubt that when history first knew of them they were Frenchmen. The whole Great West, in fact, was once as much a province of France as Canada; for the dominions of Louis XV were supposed to stretch from Quebec to New Orleans and from the Alleghenies to the Mississippi. The land was really held by savages who had never heard of this king; but that was all the same to the French. They had discovered the Great Lakes, they had discovered the Mississippi, they had discovered the Ohio; and they built forts at Detroit, at Kaskaskia, and at Pittsburg, as well as at Niagara. They planted a colony at the mouth of our mightiest river and opened a highway to France through the Gulf of Mexico as well as through the Gulf of St. Lawrence. And they proclaimed their king sovereign over all.

In Ohio they had a post on the Maumee and everywhere they had settlements at each of the forts, where there was always a chapel and a priest for the conversion of the Indians. With the French, the sword and the cross went together, but very few of the savages knew that they were either conquered or converted. From time to time they knew that companies of picturesque strangers visited their towns and promised them the favor of the French king if they would have nothing to do with the traders from the English colonies on the Atlantic, and threatened them with his displeasure if they refused. When these brilliant strangers stayed among them and built a fort and a chapel, and laid out farms, then the savages willingly partook of the great king's bounty and clustered around the French post in their wigwams and settled down to the enjoyment of his brandy, his tobacco, his ammunition, and his religion. When the strangers went away, almost as soon as they had promised and threatened, then the savages went back to business with the English traders.

The company of Frenchmen who visited our Miami Indians at their town of Pickawillany, on the head waters of the Miami River in 1749, was of this last sort. It was commanded by the Chevalier Celoron de Bienville, and it counted some two hundred Canadians and French troops, officered by French gentlemen and attended by one of those brave priests who led or followed wherever the French flag was carried in the wilderness. Celoron was sent by the governor of Canada to lay claim to the Ohio valley for his king, and he did this by very simple means. He nailed plates of tin to certain trees, and he buried plates of lead at the mouths of the larger streams. The leaden plates no one ever saw for a hundred years, till some boys going to bathe found them here and there in the wave-worn banks; but if the Indians could have read anything, or if the English traders could have read French, they might have learned at once from the tin plates that the king of France owned the "Ohio River and all the waters that fell into it, and all the lands on both sides." As it was, however, it is hard to see how anybody was the wiser for them, or could know that the king had upheld his right to the Ohio country by battle and by treaty and would always defend it.

LAN I749 DV RECNE DE LOVIS XV ROY DE FRANCE NOVS CELORON COMMANDANT DVN DETACHEMENT ENVOIE PAR MONSIEVR LE MIS DE LA GALISSONIERE COMMANDANT CENERAL DE LA NOVVELLE FRANCE POVR RETABLIR LA TRANQVILLITE DANS QVELQVES VILLAGES SAUVACES DE CES CANTON AVONS ENTERRÉ CETTE PLAQVE A LENTREE DE LA RIVIERE CHINODAHICHETHA LE 18 AOUST PRES DE LA RIVIERE OYO AUTREMENT BELLE RIVIERE POVR MONVMENT DV RENOVVELLEMENT DE POSSESSION QVE NOVS AVONS PRIS DE LA DITTE RIVIERE OYO ET DE TOVTES CELLES QVI Y TOMBENT ET DE TOVES LES TERRES DES DEYX COTES JVSQVE AVX SOVRCES DES DITTES RIVIES VINSI QVE ONT JOVY OV DV JOVIR LES PRECEDENTS ROYS DE FRANCE ET QVILS SISONT MAINTENVS PAR LES ARMES ET PAR LES TRAITTES SPECIALEMENT PAR CEVX DE RISVVICK DVTRCHT ET DAIX LA CHPELLE

This is the lead plate found at the mouth of the Kanawha River at Point Pleasant, WV, across the river from Gallipolis, Ohio.

Translation

In the year 1749, reign of Louis XV., King of France, We, Celeron, commandant of a detachment sent by Monsieur the Marquis de la Galissoniere, Commandant General of New France, to re-establish tranquillity in some Indian villages of these cantons, have buried this plate at the mouth of the river Chinodashichetha, the 18th August, near the river Ohio, otherwise Beautiful River, as a monument of renewal of possessions, which we have taken of the said river Ohio, and of all those which fall into it, and of all the lands on both sides, as far as to the sources of said rivers; the same as were enjoyed or ought to have been enjoyed, by the preceding Kings of France, and that they have maintained it by their arms and by treaties, especially by those of Ryswick, Utrecht, and Aix-la- Chapelle.

In fact, neither the battles nor the treaties between the French and English in Europe had really settled the question of their claim to the West in America, and both sides began to urge it in a time of peace by every kind of secret and open violence. As for the Miamis and their allies among the neighboring tribes, they believed that God had created them on the very spot where Celoron found them living, and when he asked them to leave their capital at Pickawillany, and go to live near the French post on the Maumee, they answered him that they would do so when it was more convenient. He bade them banish the English traders, but they merely hid them, while he was with them, and as soon as he was gone, they had them out of hiding, and began to traffic with them. They never found it more convenient to leave their town, until a few years later, when a force of Canadians and Christian Indians came down from the post on the Maumee and destroyed Pickawillany.

Celoron came into the Ohio country through the western part of New York. He launched his canoes on the head waters of the Beautiful River, as the French called the Ohio, and drifted down its current till he reached the mouth of the Great Miami. He worked up this shallow and uncertain stream into Shelby County where he had his friendly but fruitless meeting with the chief of the Miamis. After that he kept on northward to the Maumee and then embarked on Lake Erie, and so got back to Canada.

It could not be honestly said that he had done much to make good his king's claim to the country with his plates of tin and lead. He had nattered and threatened the Indians at several places; and the Indians had promised, over the cups of brandy and pipes of tobacco which he supplied them, to be good subjects to Louis XV, who was such a very bad king that he did not deserve even such subjects as they meant to be. They seem not to have taken Celoron's warnings very seriously, though he told them that the English traders would ruin them and that they were preparing the way for the English settlers who would soon swarm into their country, and drive them out.

The Indians did not believe Celoron, and yet he told them the truth. The English traders were often men of low character, thoroughly dishonest in their dealings and the English settlers were only waiting for the end of the struggle with the French to come and take the Indians' lands from them. If the French soldiers and the French priests had won in that struggle, Ohio and the whole West might now be something like the Province of Quebec as it was then. The Indians would have been converted to the Catholic faith and they would still be found in almost as great numbers as ever throughout the vast region where hardly one of their blood remains.

But this was not to be. The French built their forts with a keen eye for the strongest points in the wilderness and the priests planted the cross even beyond the forts. But all around and between the forts and the missions, the traders from our colonies, which afterwards became our states, stole into the country claimed for the king of France. At that time, there was peace between the king of France and the king of England in Europe and they pretended that there was peace between their nations in America. They were very civil to each other through their ministers and ambassadors, over there, but their governors and captains here never ceased to fight and trick for the ownership of the West.

From their forts, built to curb the English settlers, the French set the savages on to harass the frontier of our colonies, which their war parties wasted with theft and fire and murder. Our colonies made a poor defense because they were suspicious of one another. New England was suspicious of New York, New York of Pennsylvania, Pennsylvania of Virginia and the mother country was suspicious of them all. She was willing that the French should hold Canada and keep the colonies from joining together in a revolt against her, when she could easily have taken that province and freed them from the inroads of the Canadian Indians. The colonies would not unite against the common enemy, for fear one would have more advantage than another from their union; but their traders went out singly, through the West, and trading companies began to be formed in Pennsylvania and Virginia. While Celoron was in Ohio claiming the whole land for the king of France, the king of England was granting a great part of the same to a company of Virginians, with the right to settle it and fortify it. The Virginia Company sent its agents to visit the Miamis at Pickawillany a year later and bound them to the English by gifts of brandy, tobacco, beads, gay cloths, and powder.

The allied tribes, who had their capital at Pickawillany, numbered some two thousand in all. The Miamis themselves are said to have been of the same family as the great Iroquois nation of the East, who had beaten their rivals of the Algonquin nation and forced them to bear the name of women.

But many of the Ohio Indians were Delaware, who were of the Algonquin family; they were by no means patient of the name of women and they and their friends now took the side of the French against the English. When at last the West, together with the whole of Canada, fell to the English and there presently began to be trouble between the American colonists and the English king, all the Indians, both Iroquois and Algonquin took part against the Americans. A little victory for either side, however, with gifts of brandy and tobacco, would turn their savage hearts toward the victors; and one must not be too confident in saying that the Indians were always for the French against the English, or always for the English against the Americans.

In fact, one must speak mostly of the Indians in words that have a double sense. The old explorers, missionaries, soldiers, and traders all talk of nations, towns, villages, kings, half-kings, queens, and princes, but these words present false images to our minds. Calling the chief town of the Miamis at Pickawillany their capital gives the notion of some such capital as Columbus or Washington. But if we imagine the chief town of the Miamis as it really was, we see some hundreds of wigwams in straggling clusters along the banks of the river, in the shadow of the ancient woods, or in the sunshine of the beautiful meadows as the earliest white visitors to Ohio called the small prairies which they came upon in the heart of the forests. We see a large council house of bark, as nearly in the midst of the scattered huts as may be, where the Miamis hold their solemn debates, receive embassies from other tribes, welcome their warriors home from their forays and celebrate their feasts and dances. We see fields bordering the village where the squaws plant their corn and beans, and the maple groves where they make their sugar. Among the men and boys we see the busy idleness of children, all day long, except when the grown-up children go out upon a hunt or take the warpath. Sometimes we see an English trader coming with his merchandise and presents or a captive brought in to be tortured and burnt or adopted into the tribe.

The tribes in the Ohio country were far abler than those that the English first met to the eastward and they were fiercer than the fiercest which the Americans have at last brought under control in the plains of the Far West. Pitiless as Sioux and Apache and Comanche have shown themselves in their encounters with the whites in our day, they were surpassed in ferocity by the Shawnee, the Wyandot and the Miami whom the backwoodsmen met in a thousand fights a century or a century and a half ago. The Ohio Indians were unspeakably vicious, treacherous, and *filthy, but they were as brave as they were vile, and they were as sagacious as they were false. They produced men whom we must call orators, statesmen, and generals, even when tested by the high standards of civilization. They excelled us in the art of war as it was adapted to the woods, and they despised the stupid and wasteful courage of the disciplined English soldier. Till the white men studied war from them they were always beaten in their fights with the red men, and it was hardly the fault of the Indians if the pioneers learned from them to be savages: to kill women and children as well as armed men, to tomahawk and scalp the wounded, to butcher helpless prisoners. But this befell, and it is this which makes many of the stories of Ohio so bloody. We must know their hideous facts fully if we would know them truly, or if we would realize the life that once passed in the shadows of our woods.

*This is speculation by the author. In fact, the Indians in general were far "cleaner" than the white man who very seldom bathed. There have been several recorded incidents where Indians have talked about their enemies never bathing and that their scent was almost unbearable.

The region that we now call Ohio was wonderfully varied and pleasant. The many rivers that watered it cleared their space to the sky where they ran, and here and there the meadows or prairies smiled to the sun in grass and flowers. But everywhere else there was the gloom of forests unbroken since the Mound Builders left the land. The long levels that bordered the great lake at the north, the noble hills that followed the course of the Beautiful River, the gently varied surfaces of the center and the southwest, the swamps and morasses of the northwest, were nearly everywhere densely wooded. Our land was woodland, and its life, when it first became known to the white man, was the stealthy and cruel life of the forest. Where the busy Mound Builders once swarmed, scanty tribes of savages lurked in the leafy twilight, hunting and fishing, and warring upon one another. They came and went upon their errands of death and rapine by trails unseen to other eyes, till the keen traders of Pennsylvania and Virginia began to find their way over them to their villages, and to traffic with the savages for the furs which formed their sole wealth.

All is dim and vague in any picture of the time and place that we can bring before us. There are the fathomless forests, broken by the prairies and rivers; there are the Indian towns widely scattered along the larger streams throughout the whole region; there are the French posts on the northern border, with each a priest and a file of soldiers, and a few Canadian farmers and traders. Under the cover of peace between the French king and the English king, there is a constant grapple between the French soldiers and the English settlers for the possession of the wilds which shall one day be the most magnificent empire under the sun; there are the war parties of Indians falling stealthily upon the English borders to the eastward; there is the steady pressure of the backwoodsman westward, in spite of every hardship and danger, in spite of treaties, in spite of rights and promises. These are the main features of the picture whose details the imagination strives to supply, with a teasing sense of the obscurity resting upon the whole. It is all much farther off than ancient Rome, much stranger than Greece; but it is the beginning of a mighty history, which it rests with the children of this day, and their children after them, to make the happiest and noblest chapter in the history of the world. It is a part of that greater history, and I should like my young readers to remember that the Ohio stories which I hope to tell them are important chiefly because they are human stories, and record incidents in the life of the whole race. They cannot be taken from this without losing their finest meanings.

Chapter Three

Ohio Becomes English

NEITHER the French nor the English had any right to the Ohio country which they both claimed. If it belonged to any people of right, it belonged to the savages, who held it in their way before the whites came, and who now had to choose which nation should call itself their master. They chose the French, and they chose wisely for themselves as savages; for, as I have said, if the French had prevailed in the war that was coming, the Indians could have kept their forests and lived their forest life as before. The French would have been satisfied in the West as they had been in the North, with their forts and trading stations, and the Indians could have hunted, and fished, and trapped, as they had always done. In fact, the French people would often have become like them. They understood the Indians and liked them; sometimes they mated with them, and their children grew up as wild as their mothers. The religion that the French priests taught the Indians, pleased while it awed them, and it scarcely changed their native customs.

Wherever the English came, the Indians' woods were wasted and the Indians were driven out of the land. The English tried neither to save their souls nor to win their hearts. They both hated and despised the savages, and ruthlessly destroyed them. Now, when the smoldering strife between the French and English in the West burst into an open flame of war between the two nations, the western tribes took the side of those whom reason and instinct taught them to know as their best friends.

But ten years after Celoron visited Ohio, Wolfe captured Quebec and France gave up to England not only the whole of Canada, but the whole of the vast region between the lakes and the Gulf of Mexico, and kept for herself only the Province of Louisiana. The Indians were left to their fate and they made what terms they could with the English. They promised peace, but they broke their promises and constantly harassed the outlying English settlements.

At one time they joined together under the great Chief Pontiac* and tried to win back the West for themselves. The French forts had been ceded to Great Britain and garrisoned with British troops, and the allied Indians now took all of these but Detroit and Fort Pitt. In the end they failed, and then they made peace again, but still they kept up their forays along the English borders. They stole horses and cattle, they burned houses and barns. They killed men, women, and children, or carried them off into captivity. In the Ohio country alone their captives counted hundreds, though the right number could never be known, for they could easily be kept out of the way when the tribes were summoned to give them up.

*See Addendum C

It was the same story in the West that it had been in the East, and the North, and the South, wherever the savages fell upon the lonely farms or the scattered hamlets of the frontiers, and it was not ended until our own day, when the Indians were at last shut up in reservations. It was their custom to carry off the women and children. If the children were very young and hindered the march of their mothers, or if they cried and endangered or annoyed their captors, they were tomahawked, or their brains were dashed out against the trees. But if they were well grown, and strong enough to keep up with the rest, they were hurried sometimes hundreds of miles into the wilderness. There the fate of all prisoners was decided in solemn council of the tribe. If any men had been taken, especially such as had made a hard fight for their freedom and had given proof of their courage, they were commonly tortured to death by fire in celebration of the victory won over them; though it sometimes happened that young men who had caught the fancy or affection of the Indians were adopted by the fathers of sons lately lost in battle. The older women became the slaves and drudges of the squaws and the boys and girls were parted from their mothers and scattered among the savage families. The boys grew up hunters and trappers, like the Indian boys, and the girls grew up like the Indian girls and did the hard work which the warriors always left to the women. The captives became as fond of their wild, free life as the savages themselves, and they found wives and husbands among the youths and maidens of their tribe. If they were given up to their own people, as might happen in the brief intervals of peace, they pined for the wilderness, which called to their homesick hearts, and sometimes they stole back to it. They seem rarely to have been held for ransom, as the captives of the Indians of the Western plains were in our time. It was a tie of real love that bound them and their savage friends together, and it was sometimes stronger than the tie of blood. But this made their fate all the crueler to their kindred; for whether they lived or whether they died, they were lost to the fathers and mothers, and brothers and sisters whom they had been torn from; and it was little consolation to these that they had found human mercy and tenderness in the breasts of savages who in all else were like ravening beasts. It was rather an agony added to what they had already suffered to know that somewhere in the trackless forests to the westward there was growing up a child who must forget them. The time came when something must be done to end all this and to put a stop to the Indian attacks on the frontiers of Pennsylvania and Virginia. The jealous colonies united with the jealous mother country, and a little army of British regulars and American recruits was sent into Ohio under the lead of Colonel Henry Bouquet to force the savages to give up their captives.

Bouquet

This officer, who commanded the king's troops at Philadelphia, was a young Swiss who had fought in the great wars of Europe, in the service of the king of Piedmont and of the Dutch Republic before he was given a commission by the king of Great Britain. He had distinguished himself by his bravery, his skill, and his good sense. He seems to have been the first European commander to disuse the rules of European warfare and to take a lesson from our pioneers in fighting the Indians. And the year before he set out for the Ohio country, he had beaten the tribes in a battle that taught them to respect him. They found that they had no such wrong-headed leader as Braddock to deal with and that they could not hope to ambush Bouquet's troops and shoot them down like cattle in a pen. And the news of his coming spread awe among them.

He gathered his forces together at Fort Pitt after many delays. At one time a full third of his colonial recruits deserted him, but he waited till he had made up their number again and then he started at the head of fifteen hundred men on the 3d of October, 1764. A body of Virginians went first in three scouting parties, one on the right and one on the left, to beat up the woods for lurking enemies and one in the middle with a guide to lead the way. Then came the pioneers with their axes and two companies of light infantry followed, to clear the way for the main body of the troops. A column of British regulars, two deep, marched in the center with a file of regulars on their right and a file of Pennsylvanian recruits on their left. Two platoons of regulars came after these. Then came a battalion of Pennsylvanians in single file on the right and left, and between them the convoy with the ammunition and tools first, then the officers' baggage and tents, then the sheep and oxen in separate droves for the subsistence of the army, then the pack horses with other provisions. A party of light horsemen followed and last of all another body of Virginians brought up the rear. The men marched in silence, six feet from one another, ready, if any part of the force halted, to face outward, and prepare to meet an attack.

The Indians hung upon Bouquet's march in large numbers at first, but when they saw the perfect order and discipline of his army and the knowledge of their own tactics which he showed in disposing his men, they fell away, and he kept his course unmolested so that in two weeks he reached a point in the Ohio country which he could now reach in two hours, if he took rail from Pittsburg direct. But the wonder is for what he did then and not for what he could do now. His two weeks' march through the wilderness was a victory such as had never been achieved before and it moved the imagination of the Indians more than if he had fought them the whole way.

His quiet firmness in establishing his force in the heart of their country, where they had gathered the strength of their tribes from all the outlying regions, must have affected them still more. At the first halt he made on the Muskingum, they sent some of their chiefs to parley with him, but he gave them short and stern answers, bidding them be ready to bring in their captives from every tribe and family; and again took up his march along the river till he reached the point where the Tuscarawas and Waldhonding meet to form the Muskingum. There his axmen cleared a space in the forest, and his troops built a town, rather than pitched a camp. They put up four redoubts, one at each corner of the town, and fortified it with a strong stockade. Within this they built a council house, where the Indians could come and make speeches to their hearts' content and deliver up their captives. Three separate buildings, one for the captives from each of the colonies, with the officers' quarters, the soldiers' cabins, the kitchens, and the ovens, were enclosed within the fort and the whole was kept in neatness and order such as the savages had never seen, with military severity.

The tribes soon began to bring in their prisoners, each chief giving up the captives of his tribe with long harangues and many gifts of wampum, as pledges of good faith, and promises of a peace never to be broken. They said they had not merely buried the hatchet now, where it might sometime be dug up, but they had thrown it into the sky to the Great Spirit who would never give it back again. They wished Bouquet to notice that they no longer called the English brothers, as they commonly did when they were friendly, but they called them fathers, and they meant to be their children and to do their bidding like children. They made him a great number of flattering speeches and he gravely listened to their compliments, but as to the reasons they gave for breaking their promises in the past he dealt very frankly with them. He reminded them of their treacheries, and cruelties of all kinds and of their failure to restore their captives after they had pledged themselves to do so, and he said, "This army shall not leave your country till you have fully complied with every condition that is to precede my treaty with you. I give you twelve days from this date to deliver into my hands, all the prisoners in your possession, without any exception. Englishmen, Frenchmen, women and children, whether adopted into your tribes, married or living amongst you under any pretense whatsoever, together with all Negroes. And you are to furnish the said prisoners with clothing, provisions, and horses, to carry them to Fort Pitt. You shall then know on what terms you may obtain the peace you sue for."

These words are said to have quite broken the spirit of the savages, already overawed by the presence of such an army as they had never seen in their country before. One of the great Chiefs of the Delaware said, "With this string of wampum we wipe the tears from your eyes, we deliver you these prisoners. We gather and bury with this belt, all the bones of the people that have been killed during this unhappy war, which the Evil Spirit occasioned among us. We cover the bones that have been buried that they may never more be remembered. We again cover their place with leaves that it may no more be seen. As we have been long astray and the path between you and us stopped, we extend this belt that it may be again cleared. While you hold it fast by one end and we by the other, we shall always be able to discover anything that may disturb our friendship."

Bouquet answered that he had heard them with pleasure and that in receiving these last prisoners from them, he joined with them in burying the bones of those who had fallen in the war so that the place might no more be known.

"The peace you ask for, you shall now have," he said, but he told them that it was his business to make war and the business of others to make peace and he instructed them how and with whom they were to treat. He took hostages from them and he dealt with the other tribes on the same terms as they brought in their captives. On the 18th of November, he broke up his camp and marched back to Fort Pitt with more than two hundred men, women, and children whom he had delivered from captivity among the savages.

It is believed that six hundred others were never given up. The captives were not always glad to go back to their old homes and the Indians had to sometimes use force in bringing them to the camp where their friends and kindred who had come with Bouquet's army were waiting to receive them. Many had been taken from their homes when they were so young that they could not remember them and they had learned to love the Indians, who had brought them up like their own children and treated them as lovingly as the fathers and mothers from whom they had been stolen. In the charm of the savage life these children of white parents had really become savages and certain of the young girls had grown up and married Indian husbands to whom they were tenderly attached.

The scenes of parting between all these were very touching on both sides and it is told of one Indian who had married a Virginian girl that he followed her back to the frontier at the risk of his life from her people. The Indians gave up the captives often so dear to them, with tears and lamentations, while on the other hand their kindred waited to receive them in an anguish of hope and fear. As the captives came into the camp, parents sought among them for the little ones they had lost and husbands for the wives who had been snatched from their desolated homes. Brothers and sisters met after a parting so long that one or other had forgotten the language they once spoke in common. The Indians still hung about the camp and came every day to visit their former prisoners and bring them gifts. When the army took up its march some of them asked leave to follow it back to Fort Pitt and on the way they supplied their adopted children and brothers with game and sought in every way to show their love for them.

Bouquet reached Pittsburg in ten days, without the loss of a single life at the hands of the savages and with all his men in excellent health. Each day of his march he had pitched his camp among scenes of sylvan loveliness, on the banks of the pleasant streams that watered the fertile levels and the wild meadows, or wound through the rich valleys between the low hills. It would have been wonderful if his Pennsylvanian and Virginian recruits had not looked upon the land with covetous eyes. Even the fathers and husbands and brothers who had come seeking their kindred among the Indians, had seen it with a longing to plant their homes in it. Its charms had been revealed to great numbers of the people who had known of it only from the traders before, and the savage was doomed from that time to lose it, for it already belonged to the king of England and it rested with the English colonists to come and take it; or so, at least, they thought.

Chapter Four
The Forty Years' War for the West

THE French king gave up the West to the English king in 1763 but, as we have seen, the Indians had no part in the bargain. They only knew that they were handed over by those who had been their friends to those who had been their enemies and they did not consent. They had made war upon the English colonists before and now, in spite of the failure of Pontiac, and in spite of Bouquet's march into the Ohio country, they kept up their warfare for forty years, with a truce when it was convenient, and a treaty of peace when it was convenient, but with a steadfast purpose to drive the English settlers out and to hold the wilderness for themselves. It was not until long after their power was broken by the American arms in 1794 that their struggle ended in the region which ten years later became the state of Ohio.

There was misunderstanding on both sides. The Indians naturally supposed that their own country belonged to them and the colonists supposed that their eastern and western borders were the two oceans. These were commonly the boundaries which the English king had given them and when he had not been quite clear about it in his grants of territory, which he had never even imagined, they did not allow him to deal less splendidly with them than such a prince ought. He had, as we know, given the Ohio Company of Virginia a large tract of the best land beyond the Ohio even while the French still claimed the West, and he had encouraged the Virginians to believe they had a right to settle it and to fortify it. But after the capture of Quebec when the West, as well as Canada, fell into the power of Great Britain, the English king, or rather his ministers, began to change their minds about letting the colonists take up lands in the "Back Country," as they called it.*

*See Addendum A

The jealousy between the colonies grew less but the jealousy between them and Great Britain grew greater. There were outbreaks here and there against her rule and there was discontent nearly everywhere. The colonists were disappointed and embittered that the West should be treated as a part of Canada by the mother country when it ought to have been shared among the English provinces. The British government tried to hinder the settlement of the whites on the Indians' lands and though it could not keep them off altogether, it did enough to make the savages feel that it was their friend against its own subjects. In 1774, Parliament passed a law which declared the whole West, between the Ohio and Mississippi rivers, and below the Great Lakes, a part of the Province of Quebec. This was felt by our colonies to be so great an injury that it was charged against Great Britain in the Declaration of Independence, as one of the causes for separation. It was in fact an act hostile to a people of the British race, language, and religion, and it was meant not so much to help the savages, as to hurt the colonists, though it did really help the savages.

When the Revolutionary War broke out a year or two later, the British government did not scruple to make use of the cruel hatred of the Indians against its rebellious subjects. It set on the war parties that harried the American border, and when the blood-stained braves came back with their plunder, their captives, and the scalps of the men, women, and children they had murdered, they were welcomed at the British forts as friends and allies. In certain cases, to be sure, British officers did what they could to soften the hard fate of the prisoners, but the British government was guilty, nevertheless, of the barbarous deeds done by the Indians. Its agents furnished them with arms and ammunition and its ministers upheld them in the same atrocities against the American rebels as the French in their time had urged and tempted them to commit against the settlers when they were English subjects.

At the end of the Revolutionary War, the Indians were as slow to lay down their arms as they had been after the French War. In each case they fought the victors, as far as they could get at them, in the persons of the hapless backwoodsmen, their wives and children. These backwoodsmen did not change greatly in their way of life during that long Indian war of forty years. They were of the hardy English, Welsh, and Scotch-Irish stock which a generation or two in the wilderness had toughened and strengthened. They had not yet ciphered it out that one red hunter and trapper must waste the fifty thousand acres which would support the families of a hundred white farmers in comfort and prosperity. But they knew that to the westward there was a region, vast and rich beyond anything words could say, and they longed to possess it, with a hunger that was sometimes a pitiless greed and always a resistless desire. Yet it was not until the French gave up this region that they could even venture lawlessly into it. And it was not until it fell from Great Britain to the new power of the United States that the borderers began openly to press into the backwoods, singly as hunters and trappers, in families as settlers, and in whole neighborhoods as the founders of villages and towns. The pioneers felt that they were going to take their own wherever they found it, from the savages who could not and would not use it, and they were right, for the land truly belongs to him who will use it. The savages felt that the pioneers were coming to take their own from them, for in their way, they were using the land and they were right, too. All that is left for us to ask at this late day is which could use the land best and most and there can hardly be any doubt of the answer.

To understand the situation clearly, the reader must keep in mind certain dates. Celoron de Bienville visited the Miamis in 1749, and the French kept the Ohio Indians on the warpath against the English settlements to the eastward until 1763 when they gave up the West to Great Britain. Then, until 1775, the savages alone fought the settlers as the subjects of the English king. The Revolutionary War broke out, and the Indians became the allies of the British. Then, in 1783, their country was given up to the United States and they still fought their old enemies, who had not changed their nature by changing their name to Americans. In 1794, the great Battle of Fallen Timbers was fought on the banks of the Maumee and the long struggle was ended.

It had grown more and more fierce and cruel as time passed and, only three years before General Wayne won his lasting victory, General St.

Clair had suffered his terrible defeat by the Indians. Through this defeat, the power of the whites in the West was shaken as it had never been before. The savages were filled with pride and hope by the greatest triumph they had achieved over their enemies and all the settlements in the Northwestern Territory were endangered.

Perhaps I had better say seemed endangered. The Indians were really less to be feared than at any time before. They were weaker and the whites were stronger. They were striving against destiny. And though their fate was sealed with the blood of their enemies, their fate was sealed. All the chances that had favored them had favored them in vain, and neither their wily courage nor their pitiless despair availed them against the people who outnumbered them as the stems of the harvest field outnumber the trees of the forest.

Chapter Five
The Captivity of James Smith

THE stories of captivity among the Ohio Indians during the war that ended in 1794 would of themselves fill a much larger book than this is meant to be. Most of them were never set down, but some of them were very thrillingly told, and others very touchingly, either by the captives themselves or by such of their friends as were better able to write them out. One, at least, is charming, and the narrative of Colonel James Smith deserves a chapter by itself, not only because it is charming, but because it shows the Indians in a truer and kindlier light than they were often able to show themselves.

Smith was born in Franklin County, Pennsylvania, which in 1737 was the frontier of the white settlement, and he was taken prisoner in 1755, by a small party of Delawares, near Bedford, while he was helping to cut a road for the passage of General Braddock's ill-fated expedition against the French. The Indians hurried from the English border, and forced him to run with them nearly the whole way to Fort Duquesne, which afterwards became Fort Pitt, and is now Pittsburg. A large body of savages was encamped outside the post, and there Smith expected to be burned to death with the tortures he afterwards saw inflicted upon many other prisoners; but he was only made to run the gantlet. Two lines of Indians were drawn up, with sticks in their hands, and Smith dashed at the top of his speed between their ranks. He was cruelly beaten, and before he reached the goal he fell senseless. When he came to himself he was in the hands of a French surgeon. He was well cared for, and he lived in hopes of rescue by Braddock's army, which was marching against Fort Duquesne in greater force than had ever been sent into the wilderness. But while he was still so broken and bruised as to be scarcely able to walk, the Indians came in with plunder and prisoners from the scene of their bloody victory over the British troops.

A little later, Smith's captors claimed him from the French, and carried him to an Indian town on the Muskingum. The day after their arrival a number of the Indians came to him and one of them began to pull out his hair, dipping his fingers in ashes to get a better hold, and plucking it away hair by hair till it was all gone except a lock on the crown. This they plaited with strings of beadwork and silver brooches, and then they bored his ears and nose and put rings in them. They painted his face and body in different colors, hung a band of wampum about his neck, and fitted his arm with bracelets of silver. An old chief led him into the street of the village, and gave the alarm halloo, when all the Delaware, Caughnewauga, and Mohicans of the place came running, and formed round the chief who held Smith by the hand, and made them a long speech. He then gave Smith over to three young squaws who pulled him into the river waist-deep and made signs to him that he should plunge his head into the water. But Smith's head was full of the tortures of the prisoners whom he had seen burnt at Fort Duquesne. He believed all these ceremonies were the preparations for his death and he would neither duck himself nor allow the squaws to duck him. He struggled with them amidst the shouts and laughter of the Indians on the shore until one of them managed to say in English, "No hurt you," when he suffered them to plunge him under the water and rub at him as long as they chose.

By this means they washed away his white blood, and he was adopted into the tribe in place of a great chief who had lately died. He seems never to have known why this honor was done him but he was then a lusty young fellow of eighteen who might well have taken the fancy of some of his captors; and he probably fell into their hands at a moment which their superstition rendered fortunate for him.

When the squaws had done with him, he was taken up into the council house of the village where he was dressed in a new ruffled shirt, leggins trimmed with ribbons and wrought with beads and moccasins embroidered with porcupine quills. His face was painted afresh and his scalp lock tied up with red feathers. He was given a pipe and tobacco pouch and seated upon a bear skin, while one of the chiefs addressed him in the presence of the assembled warriors. "My son," so the speech was interpreted to Smith, "you are now flesh of our flesh and bone of our bone. You are taken into the Caughnewauga Nation and initiated into a warlike tribe; you are adopted into a great family, in the room and place of a great man. After what has passed this day, you are now one of us by an old strong law and custom. My son, you have now nothing to fear; we are now under the same obligations to love, support, and defend you, that we are to love and defend one another; therefore you are to consider yourself as one of our people."

A grand feast of boiled venison and green corn followed and Smith took part in it on the same terms as all the rest of his tribe and family. In due time he found out that no word the chief had addressed him was idly spoken and he began to live the life of the savages like one of themselves, under the affectionate care and constant instruction of his brethren. He was given a gun, at first, and sent to hunt turkeys but he came upon the trace of buffalo and was lured on by the hope of larger game, and so lost his way. The Indians found him again easily enough, but as a punishment for his rashness, his gun was taken from him and for two years he was allowed to carry only a bow and arrows. Once, when the hunters had killed a bear and he went out with a party to bring in the meat, Smith complained of the weight of his load. The Indians laughed at him and to shame him they gave part of his burden to a young squaw who already had as much as he to carry. At another time, he went to the fields with some other young men to watch the squaws hoeing corn. One of these challenged him to take her hoe and he did so, and hoed for some time with the women. They were delighted and praised his skill but when he came back to the village, the old chiefs rebuked him, telling him that he was adopted in the place of a great man and it was unworthy of him to hoe corn like a squaw.

Smith owns that he never gave them a chance to chide him a second time for such unseemly behavior. After that he left all the hard work to the squaws like a true Indian and guarded his dignity as a hunter. He was never trusted, or at least he was never asked, to take part in any of the forays against the white frontier, when from time to time parties were sent to the Pennsylvania borders to take scalps and steal horses. It was a sorrowful thing for him when his savage brethren set forth on these errands of theft and murder among his kindred by race and it was long before he could make the least show of returning their affection.

It was not until they gave him back some books which they had brought him from other prisoners but, had then taken from him for some caprice that he says he felt his heart warm towards them. They pretended that the books had been lost but declared that they were glad they had been found, for they knew that he was grieved at the loss of them. "Though they had been exceedingly kind to me," he says, "I still as before detested them on account of the barbarity I beheld after Braddock's defeat. Neither had I ever before pretended kindness or expressed myself in a friendly manner. But now I began to excuse the Indians on account of their want of information."

The family which Smith had been taken into did not stay long in the Muskingum country but began the wandering life of the hunters and trappers, working northward mostly, and visiting the shores and waters of Lake Erie. It was all very pleasant and full of a wild charm while the fine weather lasted, especially for the men, who had nothing to do but to bring in the game and fish for the squaws to cook and care for. The squaws made the sugar in the spring. They felled the trees and fashioned from the barks the troughs to catch the maple sap, which they boiled down into sugar. They planted and tended the fields of corn and beans. They did everything that was like work, indoors and out, and the men did nothing that was not like play or war. While their plenty lasted, it was for all. When the dearth came, every one shared it. But in this free, sylvan life there was the grace of an unstinted hospitality. The stranger was pressed to make the lodge of his host his home and he was given the best of his store. One day when his Indian brother came in from the hunt, Smith told him that a passing Wyandot had visited their camp and he had given him roast venison.

"And I suppose you gave him also sugar and bear's oil to eat with his venison?"

Smith confessed that as the sugar and bear's oil were in the canoe, he did not go for them. His brother told him he had behaved just like a Dutchman, and he asked, "Do you not know that when strangers come to our camp we are to give them the best we have?"

Smith owned that he had been wrong, and then his brother excused him because he was so young; but he bade him learn to behave like a warrior and do great things and never be caught in any such mean actions again.

The Indians were as prompt to praise and reward what they thought fine in him as to rebuke what they deemed unworthy; and the second winter that they spent in Northern Ohio, they gave him a gun again for the courage and endurance he twice showed when he had lost his way from camp. Once when he was caught in a heavy storm of snow, he passed the night in the hollow of a tree, which he made snug by blocking it up with brush and pieces of wood and by chopping the rotten inside of the trunk with his hatchet until he had a soft, warm bed. Another time, when he was looking at his beaver traps he was overtaken by the dark, and kept himself from freezing by dancing and shouting till daylight. His Indian friends honored him for his wise behavior and as they had now beaver skins enough, they carried them to the French post at Detroit, where they bought a gun for him. They bought for themselves a keg of brandy and they paid Smith the compliment, when he refused to drink, of making him one of the guards set over the drinkers to keep them from killing one another. He helped bring them safely through their debauch, but nothing could prevent their spending all they had got for their beaver skins in more and more brandy. Then they went back sick and sorry to the woods again.

The family Smith was taken into was honored for its uncommon virtue and wisdom. His two brothers, Tontileaugo and Tecaughretanego were men of great sense, with good heads and good hearts. They treated Smith with the greatest love and patience and took him to task with affectionate mildness when he transgressed the laws of taste or feeling. The Indians all despised the white settlers, whom they thought stupid and cowardly, and they expected to drive them beyond the sea. They despised them for their impiety and Tecaughretanego once said to Smith, "As you have lived with the white people, you have not had the same advantage of knowing that the Great Being above feeds his people and gives them their meat in due season, as we Indians have, who are wonderfully supplied, and that so frequently that it is evidently the hand of the Great Owaneeyo that doeth this. Whereas the white people have commonly large flocks of tame cattle, that they can kill when they please, and also their barns and cribs filled with grain and therefore have not the same opportunity of seeing and knowing that they are supported by the ruler of Heaven and Earth."

At this time the Indians were suffering from the famine that their waste and improvidence had brought upon them; and perhaps Smith might have said something on the white man's side. But he had nothing to say when rebuked for smiling at Tecaughretanego's sacrifice of the last leaf of his tobacco to the Great Spirit. "Brother, I have something to say to you and I hope you will not be offended when I tell you of your faults. You know that when you were reading your books, I would not let the boys or any one disturb you; but now when I was praying I saw you laughing. I do not think you look upon praying as a foolish thing; I believe you pray yourself. But perhaps you think my mode or manner of prayer foolish; if so, you ought in a friendly manner to instruct me, and not make sport of sacred things."

The prayer which Tecaughretanego thought ought to have escaped Smith's derision was one which he made after he began to get well from a long sickness and it was certainly very quaint. But if the Father of all listens most kindly to those children of his who come to him simply and humbly, he could not have been displeased with this old Indian's petition.

"Oh, Great Being, I thank thee that I have obtained the use of my legs again, that I am now able to walk about and kill turkeys without feeling exquisite pain and misery. I know that thou art a hearer and a helper, and therefore I will call upon thee. *Oh, ho, ho, ho!* Grant that my ankles and knees may be right well and that I may be able not only to walk, but to run and to jump as I did last fall. *Oh, ho, ho, ho!* Grant that on this voyage we may frequently kill bears, as they may be crossing the Scioto and Sandusky. *Oh, ho, ho, ho!* Grant that we may kill plenty of turkeys along the banks, to stew with our bear meat. *Oh, ho, ho, ho!* Grant that rain may come to raise the Olentangy about two or three feet, that we may cross in safety down to the Scioto, without danger of our canoe being wrecked on the rocks. And now, oh, Great Being, thou knowest how matters stand — thou knowest that I am a great lover of tobacco, and that though I know not when I may get any more, I now make a present of the last I have unto thee, as a free burnt offering. Therefore I request that thou wilt hear and grant these requests, and I thy servant will return thee thanks, and love thee for thy gifts."

Smith tells us that a few days after Tecaughretanego made his prayer and offered up his tobacco, rain came and raised the Olentangy high enough to let them pass safely into the Scioto. He does not say whether he thought this was the effect of the old Indian's piety, but he always speaks reverently of Tecaughretanego's religion. He is careful to impress the reader again and again with the importance of the Indian family he had been taken into, and with the wisdom as well as the goodness of Tecaughretanego, who held some such place among the Ottawas, he says, as Socrates held among the Athenians. He was against the Indians' taking part in the war between the French and English; he believed they ought to leave these to fight out their own quarrels; and in all the affairs of his people, he favored justice, truth, and honesty. The Indians, indeed, never stole from one another, but they thought it quite right to rob even their French allies; and it will help us to a real understanding of their principles, if we remember that the good and wise Tecaughretanego is never shown as rebuking the cruelty and treachery of the war parties in their attacks on the English settlements. The Indian's virtues are always for his own tribe. Outside of it, all the crimes are virtues and it is right to lie, to cheat, to steal, to kill as it was with our own ancestors when they lived as tribes.

Smith was always treated like one of themselves by his Indian brothers, and he had a deep affection for them. Once, in a time of famine, when Tecaughretanego lay helpless in his cabin, suffering patiently with the rheumatism which crippled him, Smith hunted two whole days without killing any game and then came home faint with hunger and fatigue. Tecaughretanego bade his little son bring him a broth which the boy had made with some wildcat bones left by the buzzards near the camp and when Smith had eaten he rebuked him for his despair and charged him never again to doubt that God would care for him, because God always cared for those children of his who trusted in him, as the Indians did, while the white men trusted in themselves. The next day Smith went out again, but the noise made by the snow crust breaking under his feet frightened the deer he saw and he could not get a shot at them. Suddenly, he felt that he could bear his captivity no longer and he resolved to try and make his way back to Pennsylvania. The Indians might kill him, long before he could reach home, but if he stayed, he must die of hunger. He hurried ten or twelve miles eastward when he came upon fresh buffalo tracks and soon caught sight of the buffalo. He shot one of them but he could not stop to cook the meat and he ate it almost raw. Then the thought of the old man and little child whom he had left starving in the cabin behind him became too much for him. He remembered what Tecaughretanego had said of God's care for those who trusted in him and he packed up all the meat he could carry and went back to the camp. The boy ate ravenously of the half-raw meat, as Smith had done, but the old man waited patiently till it was well boiled. "Let it be done enough," he said, when Smith wished to take off the kettle too soon; and when they had all satisfied their hunger, he made Smith a speech upon the duty of receiving the bounty of Owaneeyo with thankfulness. After this, Smith seems to have had no farther thoughts of running away, and he made no attempt to escape until he had been four years in captivity. He was then at Caughnewaga, the old Indian village which the traveler may still see from his steamboat on the St. Lawrence River near Montreal. He had come to this place with Tecaughretanego and his little son in an elm-bark canoe, all the way from Detroit; and now, hearing that a French ship was at Montreal with English prisoners of war, he stole away from the Indians and got on board with the rest. The prisoners were shortly afterwards exchanged and Smith got home to his friends early in 1760. They had never known whether he had been killed or captured and they were overjoyed to see him, though they found him quite like an Indian in his walk and bearing.

He married, and settled down on a farm but he was soon in arms against the Indians. He served as a Lieutenant in Bouquet's expedition, and became a Colonel of the Revolutionary army. After the war he took his family to Kentucky, where he lived until he died in 1812. The Indians left him unmolested in his reading or writing while he was among them, and he had kept a journal, which he wrote out in the delightful narrative of his captivity, first published in 1799. He modestly says in his preface that the chief use he hopes for it is from his observations on Indian warfare, but, these have long ceased to be of practical value while his pictures of Indian life and his studies of Indian character have a charm that will always last.

Chapter Six

The Captivity of Boone and Kenton

COLONEL SMITH was not the first whose captivity was passed in the Ohio country, but there is no record of any earlier captivity, though hundreds of captives were given up to Bouquet by the Indians. In spite of the treaties and promises on both sides the fighting went on, and the wilderness was soon again the prison of the white people whom the savages had torn from their homes. The Ohio tribes harassed the outlying settlements of Pennsylvania and Virginia, whose borders widened westward with every year; but they were above all, incensed against the pioneers of Kentucky. Ohio was their home; there they had their camps and towns; there they held their councils and festivals; there they buried their dead and guarded their graves. But Kentucky was the pleasance of all the nations, the hunting ground kept free by common consent, and left to the herds of deer, elk, and buffalo, which ranged the woods and savannas and increased for the common use. When the white men discovered this hunter's paradise and began to come back with their families and waste the game and fell the trees and plow the wild meadows, no wonder the Indians were furious, and made Kentucky the Dark and Bloody Ground for the enemies of their whole race, which they had already made it for one another in the conflicts between the hunting parties of rival tribes. It maddened them to find the cabins and the forts of the settlers in the sacred region where no red man dare pitch his wigwam; and they made a fierce and pitiless effort to drive out the invaders.

Among these was the famous Daniel Boone. He had heard of the glories of the land from a hunter who wandered into Kentucky by chance and returned to North Carolina to tell of it among his neighbors. Two years afterwards, in 1769, when a man of forty, Boone came to see for himself the things that he knew by hearsay, and he found that the half had not been told. But among other surprises in store for him was falling into the clutches of an Indian hunting party which ambushed him and the friend who was with him. They both escaped, and soon afterwards Boone's brother and a neighbor, who had followed him from North Carolina, chanced upon their camp. Boone's friend was before long shot and scalped by the Indians; the brother's neighbor was lost in the woods and devoured by the wolves. Then the brother went home for ammunition and Boone was left a whole year alone in the wilderness. The charm of its life was so great for him that after two years more he returned to North Carolina, sold his farm, and came to Kentucky with his family. Other families joined them, and the little settlement founded in the woods where he had ranged solitary with no friend but his rifle and with foes everywhere, was called Boonesborough.

Boonesborough

The Revolutionary War broke out and the Ohio Indians, who had hitherto fought the pioneers as Englishmen, now fought them as Americans with fresh fury, under the encouragement of the British commandant at Detroit. In January of 1778, Boone took thirty of his men, and went to make salt at the Blue Licks, where, shortly after, while he was hunting in the woods, he found himself in the midst of two hundred Indian warriors who were on their way to attack Boonesborough. He was then fifty years old and the young Indians soon overtook him when he tried to escape by running, and made him their prisoner. His captors treated him kindly, as their custom was with prisoners, until they decided what should be done with them, and at the Licks his whole party gave themselves up on promise of the same treatment. This was glory enough for the present; the Indians, as they always did when they had won a victory, went home to celebrate it and left Boonesborough unmolested.

They took all their prisoners to the town of Old Chillicothe, on the banks of the Little Miami in Greene County. What became of his men we are not told; none of them kept a journal as Smith did, but it is certain that Boone was adopted into an Indian family as Smith was. The Indians, in fact, all became fond of him, perhaps because he was so much like themselves in temperament and behavior, for he was a grave, silent man, very cold and wary, with a sort of savage calm. He was well versed in their character and knew how to play upon their vanity. One of the few things he seems to have told of his captivity was that when they asked him to take part in their shooting matches he beat them just often enough to show them his wonderful skill with the rifle and then allowed them the pleasure of beating such a splendid shot as he had proved himself. But probably he had other engaging qualities, or so it appeared when the Indians took him with them to Detroit. The British commandant offered them a ransom of a hundred pounds for him, while several other Englishmen, who liked and pitied him, pressed him to take money and other favors from them. Boone stoically refused because he could never hope to make any return to them and his red brethren refused because they loved Boone too well to part with him at any price, and they took him back to Old Chillicothe with them.

He never betrayed the anxiety for his wife and children that constantly tormented him, for fear of rousing the suspicions of the Indians; but when he reached Old Chillicothe and found a large party painted and ready to take the warpath in a new attack upon Boonesborough, he could bear it no longer. He showed no sign of his misery, however; he joined the Indians in all their sports as before, but he was always watching for some chance to escape, and one morning in the middle of June he stole away from his captors. He made his way a hundred and sixty miles through the woods and on the ninth day entered Boonesborough, faint with the fast which he had broken but once in his long flight, to find that he had been given up for dead and his family had gone back to North Carolina.

Boone spent the rest of his days fighting wild men and hunting wild beasts in Kentucky, until both were well nigh gone and the tamer life of civilization pressed closer about him. Then he set out for Missouri, where he found himself again in the wilderness, and dwelt there in his beloved solitude till he died. Nothing ever moved him so much as the memoir which a young man wrote down for him and had printed. He was fond of having it read to him (for he could not read any more than he could write), and he would cry out in delight over it, "All true; not a lie in it!" But it is recorded that he once allowed himself to be so far excited by the heroic behavior of a friend who had saved his life in an Indian fight, at the risk of his own, as to say, "You behaved like a man, that time."

This friend was Simon Kenton, or rather Simon Butler, one of the greatest of all the Indian hunters of Kentucky and Ohio. He had changed his name to escape pursuit from his old home in Virginia, when he fled leaving one of his neighbors, as he supposed, dead on the ground after a fight, and he kept the name he had taken through the rest of his life. He wandered about on the frontier and in the wilderness beyond it for several years, fighting the savages single handed or with a few comrades, and at times serving as scout or spy in the expeditions of the English against them.

Simon Kenton in 1836, age 81

When the Revolution began, Kenton sided of course with his own people and he stood two sieges by the Indians in Boonesborough. It was here that Boone found him in 1778 when he escaped from Old Chillicothe, and they promptly made a foray together into the Ohio country against an Indian town on Paint Creek. They fell in with a war party on the way and after some fighting, Boone went back, but Kenton kept on with another friend and did not return till they had stolen some Indian horses. As soon as they reached Boonesborough the commandant sent them into Ohio again to reconnoiter a town on the Little Miami which he wished to attack and here, once more, Kenton was tempted by the chance to steal horses. He could not bear to leave any, and he and his men started homeward through the woods with the whole herd. When they came to the Ohio, it was so rough that Kenton was nearly drowned in trying to cross the river. He got back to the northern shore, where they all waited for the wind to go down and the waves to fall, and where the Indians found them the second morning. His comrades were killed and Kenton was taken prisoner by the Indians whose horses they had stolen. The Indians were always stealing white men's horses, but they seemed to think it was very much more wicked and shameful for white men to steal Indians' horses. They fell upon Kenton and beat him over the head with their ramrods and mocked him with cries of, "Steal Indians' hoss, hey!"

But this was only the beginning of his sufferings. They fastened him for the night by stretching him on the ground with one stick across his breast and another down his middle and tying his hands and feet to these with thongs of buffalo skin. Stakes were driven into the earth, and his pinioned arms and legs were bound to them while a halter, which was passed round his neck and then round a sapling nearby, kept him from moving his head. All the while they were making sure in this way that he should not escape, the Indians were cuffing his ears, and reviling him for a "Thief! A hoss steal! A rascal!"

In the morning they mounted him on an unbroken colt, with his hands tied behind him and his legs tied under the horse, and drove it into the briers and underbrush where his face and hands were torn by the brambles until the colt quieted down of itself and followed in line with the other horses. The third day, as they drew near the town of Old Chillicothe where Boone had been held captive, they were met by the chief Blackfish, who said sternly to Kenton in English, "You have been stealing horses."

"Yes sir."

"Did Captain Boone tell you to steal our horses?"

"No, sir, I did it on my own accord."

Blackfish then lashed him over the naked back with a hickory switch till the blood ran and with blows and taunts from all sides Kenton was marched forward to the village.

The Indians could not wait for his arrival. They came out, men, women, and children, to meet him, with whoops and yells and when they had made his captors fasten him to a stake, they fell upon him and tore off all that was left of his clothes, and amused themselves till midnight by dancing and screaming round him and beating him with rods and their open hands. In the morning he was ordered to run the gantlet, through two rows of Indians of all ages and sexes, armed with knives, clubs, switches, and hoe handles and ready to cut, strike, and stab at him as he dashed by them on his way to the council house, a quarter of a mile from the point of starting. But Kenton was too wary to take the risks before him. He suddenly started aside from the lines; he turned and doubled in his course and managed to reach the council house unhurt except for the blows of two Indians who threw themselves between him and its door.

Here a council was held at once, and he was sentenced to be burnt at the stake, but the sentence was ordered to be carried out at the town of Wapatomica on Mad River. A white renegade among the Indians told him of his fate with a curse, and Kenton resolved that rather than meet it, he would die in the attempt to escape. On the way to Wapatomica he gave his guard the slip and dashed into the woods; and he had left his pursuers far behind, when he ran into the midst of another party of Indians, who seized him and drove him forward to the town.

A second council was now held, and after Kenton had run the gantlet a second time and been severely hurt, the warriors once more gathered in the council house, and sitting on the ground in a circle voted his death by striking the earth with a war club, or by passing it to the next if inclined to mercy. He was brought before them, as he supposed, to be told when he was to die, but a blanket was thrown upon the ground for him to sit upon in the middle of the circle and Simon Girty, the great renegade, who was crueler to the whites than the Indians themselves, began harshly to question him about the number of men in Kentucky. A few words passed, and then Girty asked, "What is your name?"

"Simon Butler," said Kenton, and Girty jumped from his seat and threw his arms around Kenton's neck. They had been scouts together in the English service, before the Revolution began, and had been very warm friends, and now Girty set himself to save Kenton's life. He pleaded so strongly in his favor that the council at last voted to spare him, at least for the time being.

Three weeks of happiness for Kenton followed in the society of his old friend, who clothed him at his own cost from the stores of an English trader in the town, and took him to live with him; and it is said that if the Indians had continued to treat him kindly, Kenton might perhaps have cast his lot with them, for he could not hope to go back to his own people, with the crime of murder, as he supposed, hanging over him, and he had no close ties binding him to the whites elsewhere. But at the end of these days of respite, a war party came back from the Virginian border, where they had been defeated and the life of the first white man who fell into their power must pay, by the Indian law, for the life of the warrior they had lost.

The leaders of this party found Kenton walking in the woods with Girty, and met him with scowls of hate, refusing his hand when he offered it. The rage of the savages against him broke out afresh. One of them caught an ax from his squaw who was chopping wood, and as Kenton passed him on his way into the village, dealt him a blow that cut deep into his shoulder. For a third time a council was held, and for a third time Kenton was doomed to die by fire. Nothing that Girty could say availed and he was left to tell his friend that he must die.

Kenton's sentence was to be now carried out at Sandusky, and with five Indian guards he set out for that point. On their way they stopped at a town on the waters of the Scioto, where the captive found himself in the presence of a chief of noble and kindly face, who said to him, in excellent English, "Well, young man, these young men seem very mad at you." Kenton had to own that they were so, indeed, and then the Indian said, "Well, don't be discouraged. I am a great chief. You are to go to Sandusky; they speak of burning you there, but I will send two runners tomorrow to speak good for you."

This was the noble chief Logan, whose beautiful speech ought to be known to every American boy and girl, and who, in spite of all he had suffered from them, was still the friend of the white men. He kept his word to Kenton, though he seemed to fail, as Girty had failed, to have his sentence set aside, and Kenton was taken on to Sandusky. But here, the day before they set for him to die, a British Indian agent, a merciful man whose name, Drewyer, we ought to remember, made the Indians give him up, that the commandant at Detroit might find out from him the state of the American forces in Kentucky. He had to promise the savages that Kenton should afterwards be returned to them; but though Kenton could not or would not tell him what he wished to know, Drewyer assured him that he would never abandon any white prisoner to their cruelty.

At Detroit, Kenton was kindly treated by the English and beyond having to report himself daily to the officer who had charge of him, there was nothing to make him feel that he was a prisoner. But he grew restive in his captivity and after he had borne seven months of it and got well of all his wounds and bruises, he plotted with two young Kentuckians, who had been taken with Boone at the Blue Licks, to attempt his escape with them. They bought guns from some drunken Indians and hid them in the woods. Then in the month of June, 1778, they started southward through the wilderness and after thirty days reached Louisville in safety. Kenton continued to fight the Indians in all the wars, large and little, till they were beaten by General Wayne in 1794. Eight years later he came to live in Ohio, settling near Urbana, but removing later to Zanesfield, on the site of the Indian town Wapatomica where he was once to have been burned and where he died peaceably in 1836 when he was eighty-one years old. He is described as a tall, handsome man of an erect figure and carriage, a fair complexion, and a most attractive countenance. "He had," his biographer tells us, "a soft, tremulous voice, very pleasing to the hearer and laughing gray eyes that appeared to fascinate the beholder," except in his rare moments of anger, when their fiery glance would curdle the blood of those who had roused his wrath. He was above all the heroes of Ohio history, both in his virtues and his vices, the type of the Indian fighter. He was ready to kill or to take the chances of being killed, but he had no more hate apparently for the wild men than for the wild beasts he hunted.

Chapter Seven
The Renegades

Simon Girty

SIMON GIRTY, who tried so hard to save Kenton's life at Wapatomica, was the most notorious of those white renegades who abounded in the Ohio country during the Indian wars. The life of the border was often such as to make men desperate and cruel and the life of the wilderness had a fascination which their fierce natures could hardly resist. Kenton himself, as we have seen, might perhaps have willingly remained with the Indians if they had wished him to be one of them, though he was at heart too kindly and loyal ever to have become the enemy of his own people, and if he had been adopted into an Indian family he would probably have been such an Indian as Smith was. But in the sort of backwoodsman he had been there was such stuff as renegades were made of. Like him, these desperadoes had mostly fled from the settlements after some violent deed and could not have gone back to their homes there if they could. Yet they were not much worse than the traders who came and went among the Indians in times of peace and supplied them with the weapons and the ammunition they might use at any moment against the settlers.

Indeed, wherever the two races touched they seemed to get all of each other's vices and very few of each other's virtues and it is doubtful if the law breakers who escaped from the borders to the woods were more ferocious than many whom they left behind. Neither side showed mercy. Their warfare was to the death; the white men tomahawked and scalped the wounded as the red men did. And if the settlers were not always so pitiless to their prisoners or to the wives and children of their warriors, they were guilty of many acts of murderous treachery and murderous fury. One of the best and truest friends they ever had, the great Mingo chief Logan, who was at last the means of Kenton's escape from the stake, bore witness to these facts in his famous speech; for in spite of his friendship for the whites, he had suffered the worst that they could do to the worst of their foes. When such white men as those that butchered Logan's kindred sided with the Indians, they only changed their cause; their savage natures remained unchanged; but very few of these, even, seem to have been so far trusted in their fear and hate for their own people as to be taken by the Indians in their forays against the whites.

The great Miami chief Little Turtle, who outgeneraled the Americans at the defeat of St. Clair, used to tell with humorous relish how he once trusted a white man adopted into his tribe. This white man was very eager to go with him on a raid into Kentucky and when they were stealing upon the cabin they were going to attack, nothing could restrain his desire to be foremost. When they got within a few yards, he suddenly dashed forward with a yell of "Indians, Indians!" and left his red brethren to get out of the range of the settlers' rifles as fast as they could.

But Simon Girty led many of the savage attacks, and showed himself the relentless enemy of the American cause at every chance, though more than once he used his power with the Indians to save prisoners from torture and death. He was born in Pennsylvania, and he was captured with his brothers, George and James, during Braddock's campaign. They were all taken to Ohio where George was adopted by the Delaware, James by the Shawnee, and Simon by the Seneca. George died a drunken savage; James became the terror of the Kentucky border and infamous throughout the West by his cruelty to the women among the Indians' captives; he seems to have been without one touch of pity for the fate of any of their prisoners and his cruelties were often charged upon Simon, who had enough of his own to answer for. Yet he seems to have been the best as well as the ablest of the three brothers whose name is the blackest in Ohio history. Many of the stories about him are evidently mere romance and they often conflict. As he was captured when very young, he never learned to read or write and it is said that he was persuaded by worse and wiser men to take sides with the British in the Revolution. But we need not believe that he was so ignorant or so simple as this in accounting for his preference of his red brethren and their cause. In fact, several letters attributed to him exist, though he may have dictated these and may not have known how to write after all.

It is certain that he was a man of great note and power among the Indians and one of their most trusted captains. He led the attack on Wheeling in 1777 where he demanded the surrender of the fort to the English king, whose officer, he boasted, was himself.

In 1782 he attacked Bryan's Station in Kentucky with a strong force of Indians, but met with such a gallant resistance that he attempted to bring the garrison to terms by telling them who he was and threatening them with the reinforcements and the cannon which he said he expected hourly. He promised that all their lives should be spared if they yielded, but while he waited with the white flag in his hand on the stump where he stood to harangue them, a young man answered him from the fort: "You need not be so particular to tell us your name; we know your name and you, too. I've had a villainous untrustworthy cur dog this long while named Simon Girty, in compliment to you, he's so like you, just as ugly and just as wicked. As to the cannon, let them come on; the country's aroused, and the scalps of your red cutthroats, and your own too, will be drying in our cabins in twenty-four hours; and if, by chance, you or your allies do get into the fort, we've a big store of rods laid in to scourge you out again."

The Indians retreated, but Girty glutted his revenge for the failure and the insult in many a fight afterwards with the Americans and in many a scene of torture and death. The Kentuckians now followed his force to the Blue Licks, where the Indians ambushed them and beat them back with fearful slaughter.

Girty remained with the savages and took part in the war which they carried on against our people long after our peace with the British. He was at the terrible defeat of St. Clair in 1791 and he had been present at the burning of Colonel Crawford in 1782. By some, he is said to have tried to beg and to buy their prisoner off from the Wyandots, and by others to have taken part in mocking his agonies, if not in torturing him. It seems certain that he lived to be a very old man and it is probable that he died fighting the Americans in our second war with Great Britain.

But the twilight of the forest rests upon most of the details of his history and the traits of his character. The truth about him seems to be that he had really become a savage and it would not be strange if he felt all the ferocity of a savage, together with the rare and capricious emotions of pity and generosity which are apt to visit the savage heart. There have always been good Indians and bad Indians and Simon Girty was simply a bad Indian.

Chapter Eight
The Wickedest Deed in our History

THE Indians despised the white men for what they thought their stupidity in warfare, when they stood up in the open to be shot at, as the soldiers who were sent against them mostly did, instead of taking to trees and hiding in tall grass and hollows of the ground, as the backwoodsmen learned to do. Smith tells us that when Tecaughretanego heard how Colonel Grant, in the second campaign against Fort Duquesne, outwitted the French and Indians by night and stole possession of a hill overlooking the post, he praised his craft as that of a true warrior; but as to his letting his pipers play at daybreak and give the enemy notice of his presence, so that the Indians could take to trees and shoot his Highlanders down with no danger to themselves, he could only suppose that Colonel Grant had got drunk over night.

The savages respected the whites when they showed cunning, and they did not hate them the more for not showing mercy in fight; but we have seen how fiercely they resented the crime of horse stealing in Kenton's case, though they were always stealing horses themselves from the settlers; and any deed of treachery against themselves they were eager and prompt to punish, though they were always doing such deeds against their enemies. Still, it is doubtful whether with all their malignity they were ever guilty of anything so abominable as the massacre of the Christian Indians at Gnadenhutten, by the Americans; and if there is record of any wickeder act in the history not only of Ohio, but of the whole United States, I do not know of it. The Spaniards may have outdone it in some of their dealings with the Indians, but I cannot call to mind any act of theirs that seems so black, so wholly without justice and without reason. It is no wonder that it embittered the hostilities between the red men and the white men and made the war, which outlasted our Revolution ten years, more and more unmerciful to the very end.

The missionaries of the Moravian Church were more successful than any others in converting the Indians, perhaps because they asked the most of them. They made them give up all the vices which the Indians knew were vices and all the vices that the Indians thought were virtues when practiced outside of their tribe. They forbade them to lie, to steal, to kill; they taught them to wash themselves, to put on clothes, to work, and to earn their bread. Upon these hard terms they had congregations and villages in several parts of Connecticut, New York, and Pennsylvania, which nourished for a time against the malice of the disorderly and lawless settlers around them, but which had yielded to the persecutions of white men and red men alike when, in 1771, the chiefs of the Delaware sent messages to the Moravians and invited them to come out and live among them in Ohio. The Lenni-lenape, as the Delaware called themselves, had left the East, where they were subject to the Iroquois, and they now had their chief towns on the Muskingum. Near the place where the Tuscarawas and Walhonding meet to form the Muskingum, they offered lands to the Moravians and in 1772 the Christian Indians left their last village in Western Pennsylvania and settled there at three points which they called Schoenbrunn, the Beautiful Spring, Lichtenau, Field of Light, and Gnadenhutten, the Tents of Grace.

It was in the very heart of the Western wilderness, but the land was rich and the savage was friendly. In a few years the teachers and their followers had founded a fairer and happier home than they had known before and had begun to spread their light around them. The Indians came from far and near to see their fields and orchards and gardens, with the houses in the midst of them, built of squared logs and set on streets branching to the four quarters from the chapel, which was the peaceful citadel of each little town. It must have seemed a stately edifice to their savage eyes, with its shingled roof, and its belfry, where, ten years before any white man had settled beyond the Ohio, the bell called the Christian Indians to prayer. No doubt the creature comforts of the Christians had their charm, too, for the hungry pagans. They were not used elsewhere to the hospitality that could set before them such repasts as one of the missionaries tells us were spread for the guest at Gnadenhutten. A table furnished with "good bread, meat, butter, cheese, milk, tea and coffee, and chocolate, and such fruits and vegetables as the season afforded" could hardly have been less wonderful in the Indian's eyes than red men with their hair cut, and without paint or feathers, at work in the fields like squaws.

Their heathen neighbors began to come into the Moravians' peaceful fold and the three villages grew and flourished till the war broke out between the colonies and Great Britain. Then the troubles and sorrows of the Moravians, white and red, began again. They were too weak to keep the savage war parties from passing through their towns and they dared not refuse them rest and food. The warriors began to come with the first leaves of spring, and they came and went till the first snows of autumn made their trail too plain for them to escape pursuit from the border. The Moravians did what they could to ransom their captives and to save them from torture when the warriors returned after their raids, but all their goodness did not avail them against the suspicion of the settlers. The backwoodsmen looked on them as the spies and allies of the savages, and the savages on their side believed them in league with the Americans.

The Delaware had promised the Moravian teachers that if they settled among them, the Delaware nation would take no part in the war and the most of them kept their promise. But some of the young men broke it, and the nation would not forbid the Wyandots from passing through their country to and from the Virginia frontier. It was true that the Moravians held thousands of Delaware warriors neutral and that our American officers knew their great power for good among the Indians; but the backwoodsmen hated them as bitterly as they hated the Wyandots. Their war parties passed through the Christian villages, too, when they went and came on their forays beyond the Ohio, and at one time their leaders could hardly keep them from destroying a Moravian town, even while they were enjoying its hospitality.

This situation could not last. In August, 1781, a chief of the Hurons, called the Half King, came with a large body of Indians flying the English flag and accompanied by an English officer, to urge the Christians to remove to Sandusky, where they were told they could be safe from the Virginians. They refused, and then the Half King shot their cattle, plundered their fields and houses, and imprisoned their teachers and at last forced them away. When the winter came on, the exiles began to suffer from cold and hunger, and many of their children died. To keep themselves and their little ones from starving, parties stole back from Sandusky throughout the winter to gather the corn left standing in the fields beside the Muskingum.

In March a larger party than usual returned to the deserted villages with a number of women and children, all unarmed, except for the guns that the men carried to shoot game. But in February the savages had fallen upon a lonely cabin and butchered all its inmates with more than common cruelty, and the whole border was ablaze with fury against the redskins, whether they called themselves Christians or not. A hundred and sixty backwoodsmen gathered at Mingo Bottom under the lead of Colonel David Williamson, who had once disgraced himself among them by preventing them from killing some Moravian prisoners, and who now seems to have been willing to atone for his humanity.

They marched swiftly to the Muskingum where they stole upon the Indians in the cornfields, and seized their guns. They told them at first that they were going to take them to Fort Pitt and at the vote held to decide whether they should burn their prisoners alive or simply tomahawk and scalp them, there was really some question of their transfer to Pittsburg. This plan was favored by the leaders and it is believed that if Colonel Williamson could have had his way, it would have been carried out. But there is no proof of this and the rest, who were by no means the worst men of the border, but some of the best, voted by a large majority to kill their prisoners.

They gave them the night to prepare for death. One poor woman fell on her knees before Williamson and begged for her life but the most of them seem to have submitted without a word. They spent the night in prayer and singing and when their butchers sent at daybreak to know if they were ready, they answered that they had received the assurance of God's peace.

Then the murderers parted the women and children from the men and shut them up in another cabin and the two cabins they fitly called the slaughterhouses. One of them found a cooper's mallet in the cooper's shop where the men were left and saying: "How exactly this will answer for the business!" He made his way through the kneeling ranks to one of the most fervent of the converts and struck him down. While the Indians still prayed and sang. He killed twelve more of them and then passed the mallet to another butcher with the words, "My arm fails me. Go on in the same way. I think I have done pretty well."

Among the women and children the slaughter began with a very old and pious widow and soon the sound of the singing and the praying was silenced in death.

The victims were scalped as they fell and when the bloody work was done, the cabins were set on fire and the bodies burned in the burning buildings. Two boys who had been scalped with the rest feigned death, and when the murderers had left them they tried to escape. One stuck fast in the window and was burned but the other got safely away and lived to tell the awful tale.

The backwoodsmen themselves seem not to have been ashamed of their work, though it is said that Williamson could never be got to speak of it. The event was so horrible that it killed the Moravians' hopes of usefulness among the Ohio Indians. The teachers settled with the remnant of their converts in Canada but the Christian Indians always longed for Gnadenhutten where they had lived so happily, and where ninety-six of their brethren had suffered so innocently. Before the close of the century Congress confirmed the Delawares' grant of the Muskingum lands to them and they came back. But they could not survive the crime committed against them. The white settlers pressed close about them. The War of 1812 enkindled all the old hate against their race. Their laws were trampled upon and their own people were seen drunk in the streets.

Some of the Christians had fallen back into heathen savagery. One of these, who was found in a war party, painted and armed like the rest for a foray against the whites, said to a Christian brother, "I cannot but have bad thoughts of our teachers. I think it was their fault that so many of our countrymen were murdered in Gnadenhutten. They betrayed us. . . Tell me now, is this the truth or not?" He had lost his children and all his kindred in that fearful carnage, and yet he could not believe his own accusations against the Moravians. He added mournfully: "I have now a wicked and malicious heart and therefore my thoughts are evil. As I look outwardly, so is my heart within. What would it avail if I were outwardly to appear as a believer and my heart was full of evil?"

Chapter Nine

The Torture of Col. William Crawford

THE slaughter of the Christian Indians at Gnadenhutten took place in March, 1782 and in May of the same year, four hundred and fifty horsemen from the American border met at Mingo Bottom, where the murderers had rendezvoused, and set out from that point to massacre the Moravian converts who had taken refuge among the Wyandots on the Sandusky. They expected, of course, to fight the warlike Indians, but they openly avowed their purpose of killing all Indians, Christian or heathen, and women and children, as well as warriors. We must therefore call them murderers, but we must remember that they had been hardened against mercy by the atrocities of the savages and we must make allowance for men who had seen their wives and little ones tomahawked and scalped or carried off into captivity, their homes burnt, and their fields wasted. The life of the frontier at a time when all life was so much ruder than now was as fierce, if not as cruel, among the white men as among the red men.

The murderers at Mingo Bottom voted whether Colonel David Williamson or Colonel William Crawford should lead them, and their choice fell upon Crawford. He seems to have been a man of kinder heart than his fellows, and he unwillingly took command of the turbulent and disorderly band, which promptly set out on its march through the wilderness towards the Sandusky country. They had hoped to surprise the Indians but spies had watched their movements from the first and when they reached the Moravian villages on the Sandusky River, they found them deserted. They decided then to go on toward Upper Sandusky and if they could not reach that town in a day's march, to beat a quick retreat. The next day they started, but at two o'clock in the afternoon they were attacked by large numbers of Indians hidden in the tall grass of the prairies and they fought a running battle till nightfall. Then both sides kindled large fires along their lines and fell back from them to prevent a surprise.

In the morning the Americans began their retreat and the Indians renewed their attack with great fury in the afternoon, on all sides except the northeast, where the invaders were hemmed in by swamps. There seems to have been no cause for their retreat except the danger of an overwhelming onset by the savages, which must have been foreseen from the start. But the army, as it was called, was wholly without discipline. During the night not even a sentry had been posted and now their fear became a panic, their retreat became a rout. They made their way as best they could through the marshes where the horses stuck fast and had to be abandoned and the men themselves sometimes sank to their necks in the soft ooze. Instead of keeping together, as Crawford advised but had no power to compel, the force broke up into small parties, which the Indians destroyed or captured. Many perished in the swamps; some were followed as far as the Ohio River. The only one of the small parties which escaped was that of forty men under Colonel Williamson, the leader of the Gnadenhutten massacre, who enjoyed the happier fortune denied to Colonel Crawford.

This ill-fated officer was tormented after the retreat began by his fear for the safety of his son, his son-in-law and his nephews and he left his place at the head of the main body and let the army file past him while he called and searched for the missing men. He did not try to overtake it till it was too late to spur his wearied horse forward. He fell in with Dr. John Knight, who accompanied the expedition as surgeon, and who now generously remained with Crawford. They pushed on together with two others through the woods, guided by the North Star, but on the second day after the army had left them behind, a party of Indians fell upon them and made them prisoners.

Their captors killed their two companions, Captain Biggs and Lieutenant Ashley the following day, but Crawford and Knight were taken to an Indian camp at a little distance and then to the old Wyandot town of Sandusky, where preparations were made for burning Crawford. He seems to have had great hopes that Simon Girty, who was then at Sandusky, would somehow manage to save him and it is said that the renegade really offered three hundred dollars for Crawford's life, knowing that he would be many times repaid by Crawford's friends. But the chief whom Girty tried to bribe answered, "Do you take me for a squaw?" and threatened, if Girty said more, to burn him along with Crawford. This is the story told in Girty's favor; other stories represent him as indifferent if not cruel to Crawford throughout. In any case, it ended in Crawford's return to the Indian camp, eight miles from the Indian town where he suffered death.

The chiefs who had been put in charge of him were two Delaware of great note, Captain Pipe and Captain Wingenund. They were chosen his guards because the Christian Indians were of their nation and the Delaware, more than any other nation, were held to have been injured and insulted by their massacre. It was Captain Pipe who refused Girty's offer, if Girty ever made it, and it was Captain Pipe who urged the death of the prisoners, while treating them with mock politeness. Nine others were brought back from the town with Knight and Crawford and Captain Pipe now painted all their faces black, the sign of doom. While he was painting Knight's face, he told him that he should be taken to see his friends at the Shawnee village, and he told Crawford that his head should be shaved, meaning that he should be made an Indian and adopted into the tribe. But when they came to the place where Crawford was to suffer, Captain Pipe threw off the mask of kindness. He made a speech to the forty warriors and seventy squaws and papooses met to torture him and used all his eloquence to inflame their hate.

The other Delaware chief, Captain Wingenund, had gone into his cabin that he might not see Crawford's death. They knew each other and more than once Crawford had been good to Wingenund. The captive now sent for the chief and Wingenund came unwillingly to speak with him, for he was already tied to the stake and his friend knew that he could not save him. The chief acknowledged the kindness that they had once felt for each other but he said that Crawford had put it out of his power to give him help.

"How so, Captain Wingenund?" asked Crawford.

"By joining yourself to that execrable man, Williamson; the man who but the other day murdered such a number of Moravian Indians, knowing them to be friends; knowing that he ran no risk in murdering a people who would not fight, and whose only business was praying."

In vain, Crawford declared that he would never have suffered the massacre if he had been present. Wingenund was willing to believe this but he reminded him that the men whom he had led to Sandusky had declared that they came to murder the remaining Moravians. No one, he said, would now dare to speak a word for him; the king of England, if he came with all his treasure, could not save him from the vengeance which the Indians were going to take upon him for the slaughter of their innocent brethren.

"Then my fate is fixed," said Crawford.

Wingenund turned away weeping, and could never afterwards speak of the scene without deep feeling.

Crawford had already undergone the first of his punishment. The savages stripped him naked and made him sit down on the ground before the fire kindled to burn him and beat him with their fists and with sticks till they had heated their rage. Then they tied his wrists together and fastened the rope that bound them to a post strongly planted in the ground with leash enough to let him walk round it once or twice, five or six yards away from the fire. Girty was present, and Crawford asked if the Indians meant to burn him. The renegade briefly answered, "Yes." Then Captain Pipe spoke, and Wingenund saw his friend for the last time. After this chief left Crawford, the Indians broke into a loud yell and began the work of torture which ended only with his death.

At one point he besought Simon Girty to put an end to his sufferings but Girty would not, or dared not.

Then Crawford began to pray, imploring God to have mercy upon him and bore his torment for an hour and a half longer with manly courage. It is not known how long his torture lasted; Knight was now taken away, and no friend remained to witness Crawford's agony to the end.

I have thought it well to recount his story, for without it we could not fully realize what the white people of that day underwent in their long struggle with the Ohio Indians. Cruelty so fiendish could never have a cause, but it cannot be denied that the torture of Crawford was the effect of the butchery of the Christian Indians. That awful deed was an act of even greater wickedness, for it was the act of men who were not savage by birth or race or creed. It was against the white man's law, while the torture of Crawford was by the red man's law. It is because of their laws that the white men have overcome and the red men have gone under in the order of mercy, for whenever we sin against that order, contrary to our law, or according to our law, we weaken ourselves, and if we continue in our sin, we doom ourselves in the end to perish.

Chapter Ten
The Escape of Knight and Slover

WHEN the Indians made a raid on the settlements, they abandoned even victory if they had once had enough fighting; as when they had a feast they glutted themselves and then wasted what they had not eaten. They seemed now to have had such a surfeit of cruelty in the torture of Crawford that they took little trouble to secure Knight for a future holiday. They promised themselves that he should be burnt too, at the town of the Shawnees, but in their satiety they left him unbound in the charge of a young Indian who was to take him there from Sandusky. It is true that Knight was very weak and that they may have thought he was unable to escape, though even in this case they would probably have sent him under a stronger guard at another time when they were not gorged with blood.

His Indian guard was armed and was mounted on a pony while Knight went on foot but Knight had made up his mind that he would escape at any risk rather than be burned like Crawford. His face had again been painted black and he had Simon Girty's word, given him before Crawford was put to death, that he was to be burned at Old Chillicothe. But he pretended not to know what the Indians were going to do with him there and he easily deceived his guard, who seems to have been a good-natured, simple fellow. Knight asked him if they were going to live together like brothers in the same wigwam and the Indian answered that they were and they went in very friendly talk.

At nightfall when they camped, Knight let his guard bind him but he spent the hours till daybreak trying secretly to free himself. At dawn the Indian rose and unbound his captive. Then he rekindled the fire at the same time fighting the gnats that swarmed upon his naked body. He willingly consented that Knight should make a smoke to drive them from his back and Knight took a heavy stick from the fire as if to do this but when he got behind the Indian, he struck him on the head with all his strength. The Indian fell forward into the fire but quickly gathered himself up and ran off howling. Knight wanted to shoot him as he ran. In his eagerness to cock the rifle he broke the lock, and the Indian escaped. He got safely to the Shawnee town where he described the fight

~ 73 ~

in terms that transformed the little doctor into a furious giant whom no amount of stabbing had any effect upon.

The other Indians, who seem to have understood this cowardly boaster, received his story with shouts of laughter. But Knight was very glad to make off with his gun and ammunition and leave them to settle the affair among themselves. When he came to the prairies he hid himself in the grass and waited till dark before venturing to cross them and by daybreak he was in the woods again. He could kill nothing with his broken gun and he lived for twenty-one days on wild gooseberries, with two young blackbirds and a tortoise, which he ate raw. He reached the Ohio River on the twenty-second day and crossed in safety to Fort McIntosh.

The tragic adventures of the Indian captives must often have been relieved by comic incidents like those of Knight's escape from his guard; but there is very little record of anything except sorrow and suffering, danger and death. Certainly in the captivity of John Slover, another of

Crawford's ill-starred and ill-willed crew of marauders, there were few gleams of happier chance to distinguish it from most histories of the sort. He had been captured by the Indians when a boy of eight years, and carried from his home in Virginia to their town of Sandusky, where he was adopted into their nation, and where he lived quite happily till his twentieth year, when he was given up to his own people. He fought through two years of the Revolutionary War and he was thoroughly fitted to act as a guide for Crawford.

After the battle, or rather the disorderly rout, he was one of those who was mired in the swamps. He left his horse there and with a few others tried to make his way to Detroit. Twice the party escaped capture by hiding in the grass as the Indians passed near them, but on the third morning they were ambushed. Two were killed, one ran away, and the remaining three gave themselves up on the promise of good treatment. They were taken to Wapatomica, where Simon Kenton was to have been burned, and they soon proved how far the promises of the savages were to be trusted.

The Indians knew Slover at once and they bitterly reproached him with having come to betray his friends. At the council held to try him, James Girty urged them to put him to death for his treason. But Slover strongly defended himself, reminding the Indians that they had freely given him up and had no longer any claim upon him. His words had such weight that the council put off its decision. In the meantime he was left with an old squaw who hid him under a bear skin and scolded off the messengers who came to bring him before a grand council of Shawnee, Delaware, Wyandot, Chippewa, and Mingo warriors. But shortly after, Girty came with forty braves and seized him. Slover was now stripped and with his hands tied and his face painted black, he was taken to a village five miles off where he was beaten as usual by the people and then driven a little farther to another village where he found everything made ready to burn him, as Crawford had been burned. He was tied to the stake and the fire was lighted. An orator began to kindle the anger of the savages but at the last moment a heavy shower of rain burst over the roofless council house where they had gathered to torture their captive, put out the fire, and drove them to a sheltered part of the lodge where they consoled themselves as best they could by beating him till midnight and promising him that he should be burned the next day. He was then carried to the blockhouse and left bound with two guards who entertained themselves, but did not amuse Slover, by talking over his probable behavior under the torture that awaited him. They fell asleep, worn out about daybreak, when Slover made a desperate effort to free himself and, to his own astonishment, succeeded. He stepped across his snoring guards out into the open air. No one was astir in the village and he ran to hide himself in a cornfield where he nearly fell over a sleeping squaw and her papooses. On the other side of the field he found some horses and making a halter of the buffalo thong that had bound him and that still hung upon his arm, he leaped upon one of them and dashed through the woods. By ten o'clock in the forenoon he had reached the Scioto, fifty miles away.

He allowed his horse to breathe here; then he remounted, crossed the river, and galloped half as far again. At three o'clock his horse gave out, and Slover left him and ran forward afoot, spurred on by the yells of the pursuers close behind him. The moon came up, and knowing that his trail could be easily followed by her light, he ran till daybreak. The next night he reached the Muskingum...naked, torn by briers and covered with the mosquitoes which swarmed upon his bleeding body. A few wild raspberries enabled him to break his fast for the first time but the next day he feasted upon two crawfish. When he came to the Ohio, just across from Wheeling and called to a man whom he saw on the island there, to bring his canoe and take him over. It is not strange that the man should have hesitated at the sight of the figure on the Ohio shore. Not till Slover had given him the names of many men in Crawford's army, as well as his own name, did the man come to his rescue and ferry him over to the fort where he was safe at last.

Chapter Eleven
The Indian Wars and St. Clair's Defeat

THE Indians and the renegades at Sandusky would not believe their prisoners when Crawford's men told them that Cornwallis and his army had surrendered to Washington; but the Revolutionary War had now really come to an end. The next year, Great Britain acknowledged the independence of the United States and gave up the whole West to them, just as France had given it up to her before.

Massachusetts, Connecticut, New York, Pennsylvania, and Virginia claimed each the country lying westward of them, but the other states denied this claim. The West was finally declared the property of the whole Union and in 1784 the first ordinance was passed by Congress for its government. It was not until 1787 that the great ordinance was passed which gave the future empire of the world to the West on terms of freedom to all men: "There shall be neither slavery nor involuntary servitude in the said Territory otherwise than in the punishment of crime."

This made the West free forever, but no law of Congress could make it safe without the consent of the savage nations which had again changed masters by the treaty of foreign powers. The war between England and America was over but the war between white men and red men raged more fiercely after our peace with Great Britain than before. The backwoodsmen took this peace for a sign that they might now cross the river from New York, Pennsylvania, and Virginia to settle in the Ohio country and they were soon there by hundreds.

It is true that the United States had made treaties with the United Tribes for certain tracts beyond the Ohio River, but the Indians declared that they had been tricked into these treaties. It is true that Congress meant to deal fairly by them so far as to drive the hard bargains with them for their lands which the white men had always driven with the Indians; but the backwoodsmen waited for nothing and the old story of surprises and slaughters, of captivities and tortures went on, with the difference that the war parties now need not cross the Ohio to take scalps and prisoners and the vengeance of the pioneers had not so far to follow them in their return to the woods.

The first white settlers in Ohio were largely the kind of half-savages who had butchered the Christians at Gnadenhutten. They built their cabins and cleared their fields on lands so shamelessly stolen that in 1785 a force of United States troops was sent to drive them out of their holdings. They seemed to go, but in reality they stayed and wherever the backwoodsman planted his foot west of the Ohio, he never turned his face eastward again.

He was unlawfully there, but from the Indian's point of view he was no more unrightfully there than the settlers who came a few years later to take up farms under the land companies authorized by Congress. If any other proof were wanting that these companies possessed themselves of land which the Indians believed they had never sold, it would appear in the fact that the first thing the settlers did was to build a stockade or high bullet-proof fence of logs with a strong blockhouse for a kind of citadel, where they might gather for safety in case of attacks from any of the wild natives of the woods about them.

The invaders were from New England, from New Jersey, from Pennsylvania and from Virginia and with their coming, nearly all in the same year, there began that mingling of the American strains which has since made Ohio the most American state in the Union, first in war and first in peace; which has given the nation such soldiers as Grant, Sherman, Sheridan, McPherson; such presidents as Grant, Hayes, Garfield, Harrison, McKinley; such statesmen and jurists as Ewing, Corwin, Wade, Chase, Giddings, Sherman, Waite. We have to own, in truth and honesty that the newcomers might be unlawfully and unrightfully in the great territory which was destined to be the great state, but it is consoling to realize that they were not unreasonably there. It was not reasonable that the land should be left to savages who must each keep fifty thousand acres of it wild for his needs as a hunter. The earth is for those who will use it and not for those who will waste it, and the Indians who would not suffer themselves to be tamed could not help wasting the land.

If the whites made any mistake, it was in allowing any man to own more land than he could use, but this is a mistake which prevails in our own day as it prevailed in the days of the pioneers and they were not to blame for being no wiser at the end of the eighteenth century than we are at the end of the nineteenth. The states consenting to the organization of the Northwest Territory meant that their citizens who had fought for the independence of the nation in the Revolutionary War should first of all have their choice of its lands and so we find Ohio divided up into the Virginia Military District, the Connecticut Western Reserve, and the Bounty Lands of Pennsylvania. But large grants were made to land companies and the innumerable acres were juggled out of the hands of the people into the hands of the speculators, as the public lands have been ever since, until now there are no public lands left worth having.

The Ohio Indians knew nothing of all this, or as little as they have ever known of the fate of their ancient homes on the frontier which we have pressed further and further westward. They held in their stubborn way that the line between them and the whites was still the Ohio River, as it had been for fifty years, and they made war upon the invaders wherever they found them. At times they gathered force for a great battle and in the first two of these battles they were the victors. But in the third they were beaten and their strength and spirits were broken.

In 1790 General Harmar* destroyed the towns of the Miamis on the Wabash but they ambushed his retreat and punished his fifteen hundred men so severely that he was forced back to the Ohio.

See Addendum B

In 1791 General Arthur St. Clair led an army against the Indians in the Maumee country, and was attacked and routed with greater havoc than the savages had ever yet made of the whites, except perhaps in Braddock's defeat.

In 1792 General Anthony Wayne set about gathering another army for the Indian campaign. He moved into the enemy's country slowly, building forts in Darke County and Mercer (where St. Clair was routed) as he advanced. In 1794, at the meeting of the Auglaize and Maumee, twenty miles from the last post, which he named Fort Defiance, he finally met the tribes in great force and defeated them so thoroughly that for sixteen years they never afterwards made head against the Americans.

At this day we can hardly imagine the dismay that the rout of St. Clair and the slaughter of his men spread through the Ohio country. He was a gallant officer, the governor of the Northwest Territory and the trusted friend of Washington. It is true that his army was largely the refuse of the Eastern States, picked up in the streets of the larger towns and lured into the wilderness with the promise of three dollars a month; that these men were badly fed, badly clothed, and badly drilled; and that they were led by a general whose strength and spirits were impaired by sickness.

But with them was a large body of Kentuckians and other backwoodsmen, skilled in Indian warfare, and eager for the red foes with whom they had long arrears of mutual injury to bring up; and the hopes of the settlers rested securely upon these. The Indians were led by Little Turtle, one of their greatest war chiefs, and at the point where General Wayne two years later built one of his forts, and called it Fort Recovery, they surprised St. Clair's troops.

It was an easy slaughter. St. Clair was suffering so much with gout that he could not move from his horse when he was helped to the saddle, and was wholly unfit to fight. Yet he went undauntedly through the battle; horse after horse was shot under him and his clothes were pierced with nine of the bullets which the Indians rained upon his men from every tree of the forest. The backwoodsmen had hardly a chance to practice the Indians' arts against them before the rout began. The cannon which St. Clair had brought into the wilderness with immense waste of time and toil, proved useless under the fire that galled the artillerymen. The weak, undisciplined, and bewildered army was hemmed in on every side, and the men were shot down as they huddled together or tried to straggle away, till half their number was left upon the field. Of course none of the wounded were spared. The Americans were tomahawked and scalped where they fell. One of the savages told afterwards that he plied his hatchet until he could hardly lift his arm.

All the Ohio tribes shared in the glory of this greatest victory of their race, Delaware, Shawnee, Wyandot, Ottawa, Chippewa and Pottawatomie. There had been plenty of game that year; they were all in the vigor and force which St. Clair's ill-fated army lacked and they lustily took their fill of slaughter.*

*See Addendum B

Many stories of the battle were told by those who escaped. Major Jacob Fowler of Kentucky, an old hunter, who went with the army as surveyor, carried his trusty rifle but he had run short of bullets the morning of the fight which began at daybreak. He was going for a ladle to melt more lead when he met a Kentucky rifleman driven in by the savages and begged some balls of him. The man had been shot through the wrist and he told Fowler to help himself from his pouch. Fowler was pouring out a double handful, when the man said, "Stop; you had better count them."

Fowler could not help laughing, though it was hardly the time for gayety. "If we get through this scrape, my dear fellow," said he, "I will return you twice as many."

But they never met again and Fowler could only suppose that his cautious friend was soon tomahawked and scalped with the other wounded. Fowler took to a tree and shot Indians till his gunlock got out of order. Then he picked up a rifle which had been thrown away and which he found his bullets would fit, and renewed the fight. It was a very cold November morning and his fingers became so stiff that he could not hold the bullets which he had to keep in his mouth and feed into his rifle from it. At one time he was behind a very small tree and two Indians fired on him at such close range that he felt the smoke of their guns and gave himself up for dead. But both had missed him and he got away from the battlefield unhurt.

Another Kentuckian, a young ranger named William Kennan, was one of the first riflemen driven back by the overwhelming force of Indians. He tried to hide in the tall grass but found that his only hope was in his heels. The savages endeavored to cut him off but he distanced all except one, who followed him only three yards away. Kennan expected him every moment to throw his tomahawk at him and he felt in his belt for his own. It had slipped from its place and he found himself wholly unarmed, just as he came to a tree which the wind had blown down and which spread before him a mass of roots and earth eight or nine feet high. He gathered all his strength, bounded into the air and cleared it while a yell of wonder rose from the baffled Indians behind him. A little later he came upon General Madison of Kentucky sitting on a log, so spent with the day's work and loss of blood from a wound that he could no longer walk and waiting for the Indians to come up and kill him. Kennan ran back and caught a horse which he had seen grazing, put Madison on it, and walked by his side till they were out of danger. The friendship thus begun lasted through their lives.

This is one of the few softer lights in the picture whose darker features we must not fail to look upon. One of the grimmest of them was the War Chief of the Missasagos,* Little Turtle, who planned the surprise, against the advice of all the other chiefs, and who merits the fame of the awful day. To the Americans who saw him then, he was a sullen and gloomy giant, who fought with his men throughout the battle, arrayed in the conspicuous splendor of a great war chief, with silver ornaments dangling from his nose and ears.

*Miami

Little Turtle

Hardly less terrible than the figure of this magnificent butcher is that of the Chickasaw warrior who accompanied the American army, to glut the hate of his nation for the Northern tribesmen. When the fight began, he said he would not stand for the Shawnees to shoot him down like a wild pigeon and he left the ranks and took to a fallen log where he fired with unfailing aim. But he could not be kept from leaving it to scalp the other Indians as he shot them and his own turn to be shot and scalped came at last.

The battle ground was covered with a thick slush from the new-fallen snow, and this made the retreat more exhausting. A poor mother, perhaps one of the soldiers' or pioneers' wives, staggered along with a baby in her arms till she fell with it. The ranger McDowell then carried it awhile for her. When he gave it back she threw it away in the snow, to save her own life and the Indians found it and took it to Sandusky where they brought it up as their own.

Two years after, when a detachment of Wayne's army camped upon the scene of the carnage, they had to scrape away the heaps of bones and carry them out of their tents before they could make their beds, and they buried six hundred skulls on the field. Such is war, and we cannot look too closely on its hideous face which is often so alluringly painted that we forget it is the face of a pitiless demon.

Chapter Twelve
The Indian Wars and Wayne's Victory

Gen. "Mad" Anthony Wayne

THE Indians who had been so well generaled and had fought so ably, failed as usual to follow up their victory by moving on the American settlements in force. They kept on harassing the pioneers in small war parties but gave the country time to send an army, thoroughly equipped and thoroughly disciplined, against them.

They made a second attack on the Americans on the old battle ground where General Wayne had built his Fort Recovery, but they were beaten off with severe loss, though in their attack they had the aid of many white Canadians and even of some British officers, or at least of men wearing the uniform of British officers.

By the treaty of 1783, Great Britain agreed to give us the whole West below a certain line, but when the time came for the surrender, she refused to yield the forts south of this line. With the bad faith of wanton power she kept her posts at Oswego, Niagara, Detroit and Mackinaw, because we were weak and she was strong. And from these points her agents abetted the savages in their war upon the American frontiers.

Just before the Battle of Fallen Timbers, where Wayne won his victory, the Lieutenant Governor of Canada marched a force of Canadian militia and British regulars into the Ohio country and built a fort on the Maumee, near the battle ground, which he held until 1796 when Great Britain at last gave up all the places she had unrightfully kept. The Indians expected this fort to open its gates to them, when they fled before Wayne's men, and were astonished and indignant at the behavior of their British friends in denying them refuge. This was not from want of ill will toward the Americans, who taunted them as they passed, and whom the garrison wished to fire upon for approaching the post in force. Sharp letters passed between the American general and the British commandant, but it ended in nothing worse and our jealous army, which remained in the neighborhood laying waste the Indian fields and villages, could not perceive that the British gave any aid or comfort to the savages.

The Battle of Fallen Timbers was fought on the 20th of August, 1794 on the banks of the Maumee, near a rising ground called Presque Isle, about two miles south of the present Maumee City and four miles from the British Fort Miami. The place was called Fallen Timbers because it was covered with trees blown down long before in a tornado. These formed a natural stronghold for the savages but Wayne had every other advantage, especially in numbers. He had almost twice as many men, well drilled, armed and clothed, while the miserable and disorderly army of St. Clair had fallen a prey to a far greater force of Indians.

On the morning of the battle, Wayne sent a flag of truce to the united tribes, offering peace, but he did not wait for its return. He met his envoy coming back with an evasive answer, and he pushed on to Fallen Timbers without stopping. As soon as he reached the battlefield, he ordered his infantry to beat up the covert of the enemy, who were hidden among the logs, brush and grass, with the bayonet and as they rose to deliver their fire. His order was carried out so thoroughly and promptly that this charge of nine hundred men began and ended the fight. Two thousand Indians, Canadian militia and volunteers fled before them and the rout was complete.

The affair was so quickly over that there was no time for the incidents of heroism and suffering which heightened the tragedy of St. Clair's defeat. At the beginning of the action, General William Henry Harrison, afterwards President of the United States, but then one of Wayne's aides, said to him, "General Wayne, I'm afraid you will get into the battle yourself, and forget to give us the necessary field orders."

"Perhaps I may," said Wayne, "and if I do, recollect the standing order for the day is, Charge the rascals with the bayonets!"

Wayne had got his nickname of Mad Anthony in the Revolution from his habit of swearing furiously in battle and now he called the Indians something more than simply rascals. We have seen how his men carried out the spirit of his instructions, and it is told of one of them who got astray from the rest that he met an Indian alone and gave him the bayonet. At the same time the Indian gave the American the tomahawk, and they were found dead together, one with the blade in his breast, the other with the hatchet in his skull.

A runaway Negro, who had followed the Kentucky horsemen to the battle, saw three Indians swimming the river from the shore where the cavalry were posted and shot one of them. The other two tried to swim on with the body. The Negro fired again with deadly aim and the only Indian left was now in water so shallow that he was dragging the bodies to land when once more the Negro fired and killed his man. Then he ran up to look at the dead men and found them so like one another that he knew they must be brothers.

A strange and romantic incident of the campaign, before the battle, occurred while three American scouts, Wells, McClellan, and Miller were ranging the woods to bring in some Indians for Wayne to question. They came upon a party of three Indians; Wells shot one and Miller another while McClellan, who was very swift of foot, ran down the third. Pursuer and pursued were both stuck in the oozy bottom of a stream and when Wells and Miller came up, they were threatening each other with knife and tomahawk. Miller had been taken captive when a child with one of his brothers; he had escaped, but this brother had remained with the savages, and somehow Miller felt that the Indian confronting McClellan was his brother. They seized him and washed off his paint; he was white; he was Miller's brother. They persuaded him, with much trouble at first, to join Wayne's army and he fought through the rest of the war on the American side.

At another time as Wells and a party of his scouts came to the banks of a stream, they saw on the opposite shore a family of savages who began to cross the river towards them in a canoe. The scouts, taking them for Indians, were about to fire on them when Wells suddenly called out that the first who fired should have a bullet through his own head. He had recognized the Indians and he said that when he was a captive in their tribe, this family had fed and clothed him, and nursed him in sickness, and treated him as tenderly as one of themselves. The backwoodsmen joined Wells in talk with his friends, urging them to do what they could for peace among their people and left them to paddle away in their canoe unharmed.

Wells had been the adoptive son of Little Turtle, who led the Indians at St. Clair's defeat, and he had fought on the side of the savages in that battle. But after it was over he foresaw that the war must end in favor of the white men and he decided to abandon his wild brethren. He spoke first with Little Turtle as they were walking in the woods together and warned him in words that a real Indian might have used. "When the sun reaches the meridian, I leave you for the whites; and whenever you meet me in battle you must try to kill me, as I shall try to kill you."

But the real Indians had not Wells's forecast and they continued the war till they were beaten by Wayne, in whose army Little Turtle might have found his adoptive son. Little Turtle was himself one of the last chiefs to yield but he came in with the rest at Greenville and one year after the battle of Fallen Timbers signed the treaty by which ninety chiefs and the deputies of twelve tribes gave up the Ohio River as the Indian border and ceded half the Ohio lands to the United States.

Little Turtle, or Moshokonoghua, as he was called in the tongue of his nation, the Miamis, lived for thirty years after signing the treaty, and then died of gout at Fort Wayne. He traveled through the Eastern States in the first years of the peace and gave people there a different impression from than received by those who knew him before the defeat of St. Clair, and saw him leading the victors in that battle. He struck all who met him as a man of intelligence and wit. He got the habit of high living and bore himself like the gentlemen whose company he loved to frequent. At Philadelphia the famous Polish exile and patriot Kosciusko gave him his pistols and bade him shoot dead with them any man who attempted to rob him of his country.

His business in the East was to interest people in the civilization of his tribe, but he had no purpose of living among the whites. In Philadelphia, he said, "When I walk through the streets I see every person in his shop employed about something; one makes shoes, another pots, a third sells cloth. I say to myself, which of these things can you do? Not one. I can make a bow or an arrow, catch fish, kill game, and go to war; but none of these things is of any use here. To learn what is done here would require a long time. Old age comes on. I should be a useless piece of furniture, useless to my nation, useless to myself. I must go back to my own country."

This was what he did and as long as he lived he was steadfast for peace, for he remembered that it would be foolish for the Indians to fight the Americans and Little Turtle was not a fool. Even before the Battle of the Fallen Timbers, he urged his people to treat with Wayne rather than fight. "We have beaten the enemy twice under separate commanders," he said, referring to Harmar and St. Clair. "The Americans are now led by a chief who never stops;* the night and the day are alike to him. And during all the time that he has been marching upon your villages, notwithstanding the watchfulness of our young men, we have never been able to surprise him. Think well of it. There is something which whispers to me that it will be prudent to listen to his offers of peace."

*This statement is error. What Little Turtle actually said was "a Chief who never sleeps." It was common knowledge that General Wayne hardly ever slept except for occasional short naps.

Chapter Thirteen
Indian Fighters

IN the long war with the Indians, the great battles were nearly all fought within the region that afterwards became our state and the smaller battles went on there pretty constantly. The first force on the scale of an army sent against the Ohio tribes was that of Colonel Bouquet in 1766. But, as we have seen, the chief object of this was to treat for the return of their white captives.

In 1774 Lord Dunmore marched with three thousand Virginians to destroy the Indian towns on the Scioto in Pickaway County. He cannot be said to have led his men, who believed in neither his courage nor his good faith, and who thought that he was more anxious to treat with the savages for the advantage of England in the Revolutionary War, which he knew was coming, than to attack their capital. This was that Old Chillicothe, which has been so often mentioned before, and here Dunmore made peace with the Indians, instead of punishing them, as the backwoodsmen expected. The feeling among them was so bitter that one of them fired through Dunmore's tent where he sat with two chiefs, hoping to kill all three. He missed, but he easily escaped among his comrades, who looked upon Dunmore as an enemy of their country and a traitor to their cause.*

*This was called Lord Dunmore's War and was actually caused by the brutal murder of Mingo Chief Logan's family by border ruffians led by Daniel Greathouse. It culminated in the Battle of Point Pleasant. Some historians believe that this event was planned by Dunmore himself and Dr. John Connolly at Ft. Pitt, then under the control of Virginia. Knowing that such an event would cause all the Indians of the Ohio country to strike the war post, they hoped to draw the militias of the two most populous colonies into a border war and give England time to reinforce her troops and put down the impending revolution. For more information on this theory see the book "A Point of Controversy" by C. Stephen Badgley published by Badgley Publishing Company.

Their spirit, both lawless and fearless, was the spirit of that race of Indian Fighters, as they were called, which grew up on the border in the war ending with Wayne's victory. It led them into countless acts of daring and into many acts of cruelty and the story of their adventures is too bloody to be fully told. But unless something of it is told we cannot have a true notion of what the life of our backwoodsmen was. We have seen what they could do when they were at their worst in the Gnadenhutten massacre; but we cannot understand them unless we realize that they not only held all life cheap but held the life of an Indian no dearer than that of a wolf.

Belmont County was the scene of two exploits of Lewis Wetzel, perhaps the most famous of these Indian fighters. One day he went home with a young man whom he met while hunting and they found the cabin burnt and the whole family murdered except a girl who had lived with them and whom the young man was in love with. They started on the trail of the Indians who had done the cruel deed and came up with them after nightfall sleeping round their campfire. The girl was awake, crying and lamenting and Wetzel had great ado to keep her lover from firing at once upon the Indians. But he made him wait for daylight, so that they could be sure of their aim and then, at the first light of dawn, they each chose his mark and fired. Each killed his Indian but two others escaped into the woods, while the lover rushed, knife in hand, to free the girl. Wetzel made after the Indians, firing into the air to draw them out of their concealment. Then he turned, loading as he ran, and wheeled about and shot the Indian nearest him. He fled again...dodging from tree to tree till his gun was reloaded, when he shot the last Indian left. He took their scalps and got home with the girl and her lover unhurt.

In 1782, together with one of Crawford's men, he fell in with a party of forty Indians about two miles from St. Clairsville. Both sides fired; Wetzel killed one of the Indians but his friend was wounded and promptly scalped while four of the Indians followed Wetzel. He turned, shot the foremost and ran on, loading his rifle. The next was so close upon him that when Wetzel turned again, the Indian caught the muzzle of his gun. After a fearful struggle Wetzel got it against the Indian's breast, pulled the trigger and killed him. The remaining two followed him a mile farther and then Wetzel shot one of them as he was crossing a piece of open ground. The last left of the Indians stopped with a yell, and Wetzel heard him say as he turned back, "No catch that man; gun always loaded!"

Wetzel had fought Indians nearly all his life. When he was a boy of fourteen they attacked his father's cabin in Virginia and Wetzel was wounded before he was taken prisoner, with a younger brother, and carried into the Ohio wilderness. One night the Indians forgot to tie their captives and the two boys escaped. Lewis returned to the camp after they had stolen away, for a pair of moccasins and again for his father's rifle, which the Indians had carried off. They followed the boys, but the young Wetzels got safely back to the Ohio and crossed the river on a raft which they made of logs.

In 1786 the settlers of Wheeling, who had been troubled by Indians, offered a purse of a hundred dollars to the man who should first bring in a scalp. A party crossed the Ohio but after some days turned back, leaving Wetzel alone in the woods where he roamed about looking for Indians. The second morning he came upon one sleeping and drove his knife through his heart. Then he went home with his scalp, and got the reward.

One of the tricks of the savages was to imitate the cry, or call, of the wild turkey and then to shoot the hunter who came looking for the bird. Wetzel was one day in the woods when this call came to his ear from the mouth of a cave, a place where several whites had been found scalped. He watched till the feathered tuft of an Indian's head appeared from the cave. The call of the wild turkey sounded, and at the same time the sharp crack of Wetzel's rifle noted the Indian's death.

It was Wetzel's habit in the autumn to go on a long hunt into the Ohio country. Once he went as far as the Muskingum, some ninety miles from Wheeling, when he came on a camp of four Indians. He crept upon them with no weapon but his knife which he drove through the skulls of two as they lay asleep. The two others struggled to their feet stupefied. Wetzel killed one of them but the fourth escaped in the shadow of the woods. When Wetzel returned and was asked what his luck in hunting had been he said, "Not much; I treed four Indians, but one got away."

These were acts of war but they were very like mere murders and one of Wetzel's exploits could hardly be called anything but murder. General Harmar in 1779 had invited the Indians to come and make peace with him in the fort near where Marietta now stands. Wetzel and another Indian fighter lay in wait for the envoys who passed from the tribes to the General and in pure wantonness, shot one. He then took refuge with his friends at Mingo Bottom where the officer sent by Harmar to arrest him, dared not even attempt it. Wetzel was the hero and darling of the border where the notion of punishing a man for shooting an Indian was laughed at. But after a while he was taken, and lodged, heavily ironed, in the fort. He sent for the general and asked him to give him up, with a tomahawk, to a large band of armed Indians present, and let him fight for his life with them. Of course Harmar could not do this but Wetzel won upon him so far that the General had his fetters removed, leaving only the manacles on his wrists and allowed him to walk about outside the fort. He made a sudden dash for the woods; the guards fired upon him, but Wetzel got safely away and at a distant point he reached the Ohio. He could not swim, with his hands in irons, but by good luck he saw a friend on the Virginia shore who came in answer to his signs and set him over in his canoe. Later the soldiers found him in a tavern at Marysville and arrested him again. He was taken to the fort at Cincinnati, where Harmar was now in command, but he was released by a judge of the court just in time to save the fort from an attack by the backwoodsmen who were furious that Wetzel should be so persecuted simply for killing an Indian.

One of the stories told of Wetzel's skill in Indian warfare relates to an adventure he had after his escape from hanging by the soldiers. He was coming home at the end of a hunt in the Ohio woods when he saw an Indian lifting up his gun to fire. Each sprang behind a tree and each waited patiently for the other to expose himself. At last Wetzel put his bearskin cap on his ramrod and pushed it a little beyond the edge of his shelter. The Indian took it for his enemy's head and fired. Before he could load again Wetzel was upon him and his end had come.

It is not easy for us at this day to understand how a man, so blood-stained as this should be by no means the worst man of the border. Wetzel is said to have been even exemplary in his life apart from his Indian killing, which, indeed was accounted no wrong, but rather a virtue by his savage white friends. In person he might well take their rude fancy. He was tall, full-chested, and broad-shouldered. His dark face was deeply pitted with smallpox. His hair, which he was very proud of, fell to his knees when loose. His black eyes, when he was roused, shone with dangerous fire. He was silent and shy with strangers, but the life of any party of comrades. It is not certainly known how or where he died. Some say that he went South and ended his stormy life quietly at

Natchez, others that he went West and remained a woodsman to the last, hunting wild beasts and killing wild men.

Lewis Wetzel had two brothers only less famous than himself in the backwoods warfare and more than once Indian fighting seems to have run in families.

Adam Poe and Andrew Poe were brothers whose names have come down in the story of deadly combats with the savages. They are most renowned for their heroic struggle with a party of seven Wyandot near the mouth of Little Yellow Creek, in 1782. The Wyandot, led by a great warrior named Big Foot, had fallen suddenly on a settlement just below Fort Pitt, killed one old man in his cabin and had begun their retreat with what booty they could gather.

Eight borderers, the two Poes among them, followed in hot haste across the river into the Ohio country where the next morning Andrew Poe came suddenly on Big Foot and a small warrior talking together by their raft at the water's edge. They stood with their guns cocked and Poe aimed at Big Foot but his piece missed fire. The Indians turned at the click of the lock and Poe, who was too close to them for any chance of escape, leaped upon them both and threw them to the ground together. The little warrior freed himself and got his tomahawk from the raft to brain Poe, whom he left in deadly clutch with Big Foot. Twice he struck but Poe managed each time, by twisting and dodging, to keep his head away from the hatchet and as the warrior struck the third time, Poe, though badly hurt on the arm by one of his blows, wrenched himself free from Big Foot, caught up one of the Indians' guns and shot the little warrior through the breast.

Then Big Foot seized him again and they floundered together into the water where each tried to drown the other. Poe held Big Foot under the water so long that he thought he must be dead but the moment he loosed his hold upon his scalp lock, the Wyandot renewed the fight. They presently found themselves in water beyond their depths and let go to swim for their lives. The Indian reached the shore first and got hold of one of the guns to shoot Poe, but luckily for Poe, it was the gun he had fired in killing the little warrior.

Adam had heard the shot and he now came hurrying up. His gun was empty too, and it was a question whether he or Big Foot should load first. He shot the Indian as he was lifting his gun to fire. But Big Foot was not killed and Andrew shouted to Adam not to mind him, but to keep the Indian from rolling himself into the water. Big Foot was too quick for them. He got into the current, which whirled him away and so saved his scalp in death. About the same time another of the party who came up took Andrew Poe for an Indian and shot him in the shoulder. Poe got well of his wounds and lived for many years, proud of his fight with Big Foot who was a generous foe, and had often befriended white captives among his tribe.

It is told of Adam Poe that five Indians, all rather drunk, once came to his cabin and tried to force the door open. He sent his wife with the children out into the cornfield behind the house, remarking, "There is a fight and fun ahead." But when he saw the state the Indians were in, he did not fire at them. He fell upon them with his fists, knocked them all down and then threw them one after another over the fence and the fun was ended.

One of the hunters detailed from Wayne's command to supply the officers with game while the army lay at Greenville in 1793 was the Indian fighter Josiah Hunt, who died a peaceful Methodist many years afterwards. When he passed a winter in the woods he had to build a fire to keep from freezing and yet guard against letting the slightest gleam of light be seen by a prowling foe. So he dug a hole six or seven inches deep with his tomahawk, filled it with the soft lining of dead oak bark and with his flint started a fire. He left two holes at the edges to breathe the flame then covered the pit with earth, spread brush over it, and seated himself on the heap with his blanket drawn over his head and dozed through the night. The Indians had a great honor and admiration for him, and when they came to make peace at Greenville, after Fallen Timbers, they all wanted to see Captain Hunt. "Great man, Captain Hunt," they said. "Great warrior — good hunting man — Indian no can kill," and they told him they had tried to find out the secret of his fire and catch him off his guard so that they could get his scalp, which they felt would have been the highest distinction they could have achieved, next to getting General Wayne's scalp.

He was indeed both hunted and hunter. He never fired at a deer without first putting a bullet in his mouth to reload for an Indian who might be about to fire on him. When he skinned a deer, he planted his back against a tree and stood his rifle by his side. From time to time he stopped and listened for the slightest noise that hinted danger.

His life had its disappointments as well as its perils. Once he saw three Indians whom he might easily have killed at one shot if he could have got them in range, but they persisted in walking Indian file. If he fired and killed only one, the other two would have killed him so he was obliged to let them all go.

Captain Hunt was a quiet, modest man, very frank and sincere, and seems never to have boasted of his exploits. We have no means of knowing whether he was glad or sorry that those Indians got away in safety. Probably he was not very glad for though the fighters on both sides could admire, they could never spare one another.

The Indian fighters were commoner in the southern and eastern parts of Ohio than in the north but there was at least one whose chief exploit had the north for its scene. Captain Samuel Brady, in 1780, gathered a number of his neighbors and pursued a retreating war party of Indians from the Ohio as far as the Cuyahoga, near Ravenna. Here he found that the savages far outnumbered his force and he decided that it would be better for him to retreat in his turn and he bade each of his men look out for himself.

He discovered that the Indians were pressing him hard with the purpose of taking him alive and glutting many an old grudge against him by torture. But he knew his ground for he had often hunted there with them in friendlier days and he saw a chance for his life at a point where another man would have despaired. This was where the river narrowed to a gorge twenty feet wide, with walls of precipitous rock. As he neared this chasm in his flight, Brady gathered himself for the leap and cleared it. He caught at some low bushes where he alighted and pulled himself up the steep, while the Indians stood stupefied. They had now no hope of taking him alive and they all fired upon him. One bullet wounded him badly in the hip but he managed to swim a pond, which he came to, and to hide himself behind a log near the shore. When the Indians came up and saw the blood on its surface they decided that he was drowned and gave up the chase. Some of them stood on the very log that hid him while they talked over his probable fate and then they left him to make his long way home unmolested.

Duncan McArthur, an early governor of Ohio, though not an Indian fighter like these others, was in many fights with the Indians. In the summer of 1794 he was hunting deer in the hills near the mouth of the Scioto when two Indians, fully armed, came in sight. McArthur was waiting for the deer behind a screen or blind near the salt lick which they frequented and he took aim at one of the Indians and shot him. The other did not stir till McArthur broke from his cover and ran. He plunged heedlessly into the top of a fallen tree and before he could disentangle himself, he heard the crack of the Indian's rifle, and the bullet hissed close to his ear. He freed himself and ran, followed now by several other Indians, but he managed to distance them all and reached the Ohio River in safety.

It was war to the death between the red and white borderers. Neither spared the other, except in some rare mood of caprice or pity. A life granted on either side meant perhaps many lives lost and the foes vied with one another in being the first to shed the blood which seems, as you read their savage annals, to stain every acre of the beautiful Ohio country.

Chapter Fourteen
Later Captivities

THE Indians seem to have kept on carrying the whites into captivity to the very end of the war which closed with the Greenville treaty of 1795. As they had always done, they adopted some of them into their tribes and devoted others to torture. Nothing more clearly shows how little they realized that their power was coming to an end and that they could no longer live their old life, or follow their immemorial customs.

The first captive in Ohio, of whom there is any record, was Mary Harris. She had been stolen from her home in New England when a child, by the French Indians and was found at White Woman Creek in Coshocton County about the year 1750. When the last captive was taken is not certainly known, but two white boys were captured as late as 1791 and one of these was adopted by the Delawares in Auglaize County. His name was Brickell, and he was carried off from the neighborhood of Pittsburg when nine years old. He wrote a narrative of his life among the Indians and gave an account of his parting with them which is very touching. After the first exchange of prisoners Brickell was left because there was no Indian among the whites to exchange for him but later his adoptive father went with him to Fort Defiance and gave him up. Brickell had hunted with the rest of the children and shared in all their sports and pleasures and they now clung about him crying, when their father told them he must go with him to the fort. They asked him if he was going to leave them and he could only answer that he did not know. At the fort his Indian father, Whingy Pooshies, bade him stand up before the officers, and then spoke to him.

"My son, these are men the same color as yourself and some of your kin may be here, or, they may be a great way off. You have lived a long time with us. I call on you to say if I have not been a father to you, if I have not used you as a father would a son."

"You have used me as well as a father could use a son," said Brickell.

"I am glad you say so," Whingy Pooshies returned. "You have lived long with me; you have hunted for me; but your treaty says you must be free. If you choose to go with the people of your own color, I have no right to say a word; if you choose to stay with me, your people have no right to speak. Now reflect on it, and take your choice, and tell us as soon as you make up your mind."

Brickell says that he thought of the children he had left crying and of all the Indians whom he loved; but he remembered his own people at last, and he answered, "I will go with my kin."

Then Whingy Pooshies said, "I have reared you; I have taught you to hunt; you are a good hunter; you are better to me than my own sons. I am now getting old and I cannot hunt. I thought you would be a support to my old age. I leaned on you as on a staff. Now it is broken; you are going to leave me; and I have no right to say a word, but I am ruined."

He sank into his seat, weeping and Brickell wept too. Then they parted and never saw each other again.

One of the later captivities was that of Israel Donolson who has told the story himself. The night before he was captured, he says that he dreamed of Indians and took it as a sign of coming trouble but in the morning, the 22d of April, 1791, he went prospecting for land with another young surveyor named Lytte and a friend named Tittle. They worked together along the Ohio River in Adams County till they came to one of the ancient works of the Mound Builders. The surveyors were joking Tittle and telling him what a fine place that would be for him to build his house when they saw a party of Frenchmen in two canoes. The

Frenchmen turned out to be Indians who landed and instantly gave chase to the white men. Donolson tripped and fell and three warriors were quickly upon him. He offered no resistance; they helped him up, and had leisure to secure him in full sight of the blockhouse on the Kentucky shore where they could all see men moving about, but Donolson could not call to them for help. His captors pushed off with him northward. The next morning it rained, and one of the Indians took Donolson's hat. He complained to a large warrior, who gave him a blanket cap and helped him through the swollen streams. When they killed a bear and wanted to make their captive carry the meat, he flung it down and then his big friend carried it for him.

One day an Indian, while they were resting, built a little fence of sticks and planted some grains of corn inside of it saying, "Squaw!" as a hint to Donolson that he should be put to work with the women. When they got to the Shawnee camp, they dressed his hair in Indian fashion and put a tin jewel in his nose and upon the whole they treated him kindly enough. But almost every day he saw war parties setting off for Kentucky or coming back with scalps and horses and he was always watching for a chance to escape.

One night he encamped with two guards who had bound him as usual with a rope of bark. He gnawed at it all night long and just at daybreak he freed himself. After his first dash he stopped to put on his moccasins and knew that he was missed by the terrific yells that the Indians were giving. He ran on and to hide his trail kept as much as he could on fallen trees. At ten o'clock he hid between two logs and slept till dark; then he started again and passed that night in a hollow tree. The day following he came to the Miami River, and tried to drift down its current on a raft which he made of logs tied together with bark but he was soon forced to the shore again. He broke his long fast on two eggs he found in a wild turkey's nest. They proved to have each two yolks and he made them last for two days. In the woods, he caught a horse and tried to ride it with a bark halter but the halter rubbed a sore on its lip and the horse threw him and hurt him so badly that he lay insensible for a time; then he rose up and pressed on, but very slowly, for his feet were full of thorns. The twelfth day after his capture he heard the sound of an ax and found himself in the neighborhood of Fort Washington, or Cincinnati.

In 1793, the year before Wayne's victory, Andrew Ellison was taken by the Indians in a clearing near his cabin in Adams County and was hurried off before his family knew that anything had happened. They roused the neighborhood and the Indians were hotly pursued, but they got away with their prisoner and made swiftly off to Upper Sandusky, where they forced him to run the gantlet. He was a heavy man, not fleet of foot, and he was terribly beaten but he got through alive and at Detroit a British officer ransomed him for a hundred dollars. By that time prisoners must have been getting cheap; it was perhaps more and more difficult to hold them.

Two boys, John Johnson, thirteen years old and Henry Johnson, eleven, were captured in 1788 near their home at Beach Bottom in Monroe County. They were cracking nuts in the woods and when the Indians came upon them the boys thought that they were two of their neighbors. They were seized and hurried away, one Indian going before and one following the boys who told them their father treated them badly and tried to make their captors believe they were glad to be leaving home. The Indians spent the day in a vain attempt to steal horses and stopped to pass the night only four miles from the place where they had taken the boys. After supper they lay down with the prisoners between them and when they supposed the boys were asleep one of the Indians went and stretched himself on the other side of the fire. Presently he began snoring and John rose, cocked one of the guns and left it with Henry aimed at this Indian's head, while he took his station with a tomahawk held over the head of the other. Henry fired and John struck at the same time. Neither Indian was killed at once, but both were too badly hurt to prevent the boys' escape and the brothers found their way to the settlement by daybreak. The neighbors who returned to their camp with them found the body of the Indian who had been tomahawked but the other had vanished. Years afterward, a skeleton with a gun was discovered in the woods where he must have crept after he was shot.

In the autumn of 1792 Samuel Davis and William Campbell set out from Massie's Station, now Manchester, to trap beaver on the Big Sandy. One night as they lay asleep beside their camp fire they were roused by a voice saying in broken English, "Come, come; get up, get up!" and they woke to find themselves in the clutches of a large party of Indians returning from a raid into Virginia. The Indians bound their captives and started, driving before them a herd of stolen horses. They crossed the Ohio country and pushed on toward Sandusky, for they were Shawnees. At night they tied each prisoner with buffalo thongs and made these fast to the waist of two Indians who lay down one on either side of him and quieted him with blows if he became restive. At daylight the captives were untied but they were warned that they would be instantly killed if they attempted to escape. Davis was in dread of being burned at Sandusky and as the Indians, encumbered with their booty, made only ten or twelve miles a day, the terror had full time to grow upon him. At last one morning, just before dawn, he woke one of the Indians beside him and asked to be untied. He was answered with a blow of the savage's fist. He waited a moment and then woke the other guard, who lifted his head and seeing some of his people building a fire, released Davis.

It was still too dark for any of them to get a good shot at him if he made a dash from their midst and Davis decided to try for life and liberty. He knocked a large warrior before him into the fire, bounded over him, burst through the group around him and before they could seize their rifles, which were all stacked together, he had vanished in the shadows of the forest. They followed him, whooping and yelling but none could draw a bead on him and not a shot was fired. One Indian was so near that Davis fancied he felt his grasp at times, but he fell behind, and Davis kept on. When he had distanced them all, he stopped to tear up his waistcoat and wrap his feet, naked and bleeding from the sharp stones which had cut them in his wild flight and then hurried on toward the Ohio.

Three days without food or fire, in the cold of the early winter passed before he reached the river eight or ten miles below the mouth of the Scioto. He then saw a large boat coming down the stream but his troubles did not end with this joyful sight. One of the dreadful facts of the dreadful time was the frequent deception of boatmen by Indians and renegades who pretended to be escaping prisoners and who lured them to their destruction by piteous appeals for help. The boatmen now refused to land for Davis. They told him they had heard too many stories like his and they kept on down the stream, while he followed wearily along the shore. At last he entreated them to row in a little nearer so that he could swim out to them. They consented to this and he plunged into the icy water and was taken on board just as his strength was spent.

In 1782, John Alder, then a child of eight years, was captured in Wythe County, Virginia, by a party of Mingo who at the same time wounded and killed his brother. They already had two prisoners, Mrs. Martin, the wife of a neighbor and her little one four or five years old; it proved troublesome on their rapid march across the Ohio country to their village on Mad River and they tomahawked and scalped it.

The next morning little Alder was somewhat slow in rising from his breakfast when bidden and on the ground he saw the shadow of an arm with a lifted tomahawk. He glanced upward and found an Indian standing over him who presently began to feel of Alder's thick black hair. He afterwards confessed that he had been about to kill him, but when he met his pleasant smile he could not strike and then he thought that a boy with hair of that color would make a good Indian and so spared him.

At the Mingo village, Alder was made to run the gantlet between lines of children armed with switches but he was not much hurt and he was now taken into the tribe. He was given to a Mingo family and the mother washed him and dressed him in the Indian costume. They were kind to him but for a month he was very homesick and used to go every day to a large walnut tree near the town and cry for the friends and home he had lost.

After he had learned the Mingo language he began, in time, to be more contented. He had no complaint to make of any of the family except one sister who despised him as a prisoner and treated him like a slave. Another sister and her husband were his special friends and he relates that when he used to sit up with the Indians round their camp fire, listening to their stories, he would sometimes drowse, then this gentle sister and her husband would take him up in their arms and carry him to bed and he would hear them saying, "Poor fellow! We have sat up too long for him and he has fallen asleep on the cold ground."

About a year after he was adopted, Alder met that poor mother, whose little one the Indians had cruelly murdered before her eyes. "When she saw me, she came smiling, and asked if it was me. I told her it was. She asked me how I had been. I told her I had been very unwell for I had had fever and ague for a long time. So she took me off to a log and there we sat down and she combed my head and asked a great many questions about how I lived and if I didn't want to see my mother and little brothers. I told her I should be glad to see them but never expected to see them again. We took many a cry together and when we parted, took our last and final farewell for I never saw her again."

Alder always remained delicate and could not thrive on the Indians' fare of meat and hominy with no bread or salt; of sugar and honey there was plenty; but he missed the things he was used to at home. When he grew older he was given a gun and sent hunting and whenever he came back with game the Indians praised his skill and promised him he should be a great hunter some day.

He continued with them until the peace of 1795 which followed Wayne's victory and even then, he stayed for a time in the region where he had dwelt so long. He had married a squaw and had become a complete Indian so that the first settlers in his neighborhood had to teach him to speak English. But he did not live happily with his Indian wife; they agreed to part, and then Alder thought of going back to his own people.

He reached the house of one of his brothers in the neighborhood of his old home one Sunday afternoon and found several of his brothers and sisters there, and his mother with them. They could scarcely be persuaded that it was their son and brother come back to them and he had to tell them of some things that no one else could know before they would believe him. His old, white-haired mother whom he remembered in her youth with a "head as black as a crow," was the first to take him in her arms and she said, as she wept over him, "How you have grown! I dreamed that you had come to see me but you was a little *ornery-looking* fellow and I would not own you for my son; but now I find I was mistaken, that it is entirely the reverse and I am proud to own you for my son."

In 1792, Moses Hewit was taken near Neil's Station, on the Little Kanawha, by three Indians, who at once pushed off with him towards Sandusky. They used him very kindly and shared fully with him the wild honey which they found in the bee trees and invited him to take part in their foot races and other sports. He found that he could outrun two of them and he resolved to try for his liberty, though he kept a cheerful outside with them and seemed contented with his lot. One day they left him tied hand and foot and fastened to two small trees while they went on a hunt but he contrived to free himself and made his escape with their whole stock of provisions, two small pieces of venison. He struck out for the settlements on the Muskingum, and the first night his captors passed so near him in pursuit that he might have touched them in the darkness.

Nine days later he came in sight of a station on the Muskingum so spent with hunger and fatigue that he could not halloo to the garrison. He had nothing on his wasted and bleeding body, which was all torn by briers and brushwood, except a cloth about his loins and he was afraid of being mistaken and shot for an Indian. He waited till nightfall and then crept to the station where his presence was unknown till a young man of his acquaintance caught sight of his face in the firelight, and called out, "Here is "Hewit!"

Captain Charles Builderback and his wife were surprised by a party of Indians while they were looking for cattle in the Ohio country near Wheeling, in 1789. Mrs. Builderback hid herself but the Indians had captured her husband and now they forced him to call out to her. She hesitated to answer, thinking of the children they had left at home in the cabin which she could see across the river and knowing how useless it would be to give herself up. But he called again, saying that if she surrendered, it might save his life. Then she showed herself and was seized and hurried away by one band of savages while her husband remained with the others. A few days later these came up and showed her his scalp. He was one of the assassins of the Gnadenhutten Indians and he was doomed as soon as they knew his name. She was taken to their towns on the Great Miami where she lived nine months, drudging with the squaws and suffering from the rude and filthy life of the savages but not ill-treated. Then the commandant at Cincinnati ransomed her and sent her home to her two orphan children.

So lately as 1812 two little girls were stolen from their fathers' houses in Preble County by the Indians. They could not be traced but twenty-five years later, one of them, named Parker, was found living with her savage husband in Indiana. She refused then to go home with her father saying coldly that she should be ridiculed there for her Indian customs.

Chapter Fifteen
Indian Heroes and Sages

THE Ohio Indians were of almost as mixed origin as the white people of Ohio and if they had qualities beyond those of any other group of American savages. It was from much the same causes which have given the Ohioans of our day distinction as citizens. They made the Ohio country their home by a series of chances and they defended it against the French, the English and Americans in turn, because it had bounds which seemed to form the natural frontier between them and the Europeans.

It is now believed that before the coming of our race there was a balance of power between those two great North American nations, the Iroquois and the Algonquins, and that our wars and intrigues destroyed this balance which was never restored and put an end to all hope of advance in the native race. Whether this is true or not, it is certain that the hostilities between the tribes raged down to our day and that these seem to have continued if not begun through one family, the Algonquins, siding with the French, and the other family, the Iroquois, siding with the English. The Algonquins were most powerful in New England and Canada and the Iroquois in New York. Their struggle ended in the overthrow of the Algonquins in the regions bordering on the English colonies where, as has been told, a great branch of that people who called themselves the Lenni-lenape and whom we called the Delaware, dwelt in a sort of vassalage to the Iroquois.

In Ohio, however, these families, so long broken elsewhere by their feuds, united in a common fear and hate of the white men. Many of the Ohio Indians were Delaware, but the Miami were Iroquois while the Wyandot again were Huron, one of the finest and ablest of the Iroquois nation. They ceased to make war upon each other and in their union the strongest traits of both were blended. Their character appears at its best, I think, in Tecaughretanego, the adoptive brother of James Smith and in the great Mingo chief, Logan.

Of Tecaughretanego, his unselfishness, his piety, his common sense, his wisdom, we already know something from Smith's narrative, which I wish every boy and girl might read; and of Logan's noble spirit we have had a glimpse in the story of Kenton's captivity. He was the son of

Shikellamy, a Cayuga chief who lived at Shamokin, Pennsylvania, and who named him after James Logan, the Secretary of the Province. Shikellamy was a convert of the Moravian preachers and it is thought that Logan himself was baptized in the Christian faith. He spent the greater portion of his early life in Pennsylvania and he took no part in the war between the French and English except to do what he could for peace. When he came to Ohio, he dwelt for a time at Mingo Bottom in Jefferson County, the rendezvous of the assassins who marched against Gnadenhutten under Williamson and of the assassins who were beaten back from Sandusky under Crawford. Here, as before, Logan was the friend of the white man and it was not till the murder of his father, brother, and sister, cried to him for vengeance, that he made war upon them.

His kindred were of a small party of Indians whom some Virginians lured across the Ohio near the mouth of Yellow Creek in 1774. On the Virginia side the murderers made three of the Indians drunk and tomahawked them and when they had tricked the others into discharging their guns at a mark and so had them defenseless, they ruthlessly shot them down. Logan's sister, who was the only woman in the party, tried to escape but a bullet cut short her flight and she died praying her murderers to have mercy on the babe she held in her arms. They spared it, and he who tells the cruel tale saw it the next day in his own mother's arms smiling up into her face, while she fed and fondled it.

The news came to Logan while he was speaking at a council of the Indians and urging them to make peace with the whites. He instantly changed his plea. He lifted up his hatchet and vowed never to lay it down till he had avenged himself tenfold. He kept his word, and that summer thirty scalps and prisoners bore witness to his fury.

But it was a short-lived impulse of a nature essentially so good that it could not long keep the memory of even such an injury. In this very war, or this outburst of the long Indian war, Logan showed himself as before the friend of the white men. He had pity on many of the captives he made and when he could he tried to move other captors to pity. Major William Robinson, who was one of Logan's prisoners, tells how he was surprised, together with two friends, by a party of Indians who fired on them. Robinson ran with a savage in hot chase behind him, who called to him in English, "Stop; I won't hurt you."

"Yes, you will," Robinson retorted.

"No, I won't," the Indian insisted; "but if you don't stop, I'll shoot you." Robinson fell over a log, and the Indian seized him. It was Logan, who told him not to be frightened for he should be adopted into his own tribe when they reached his village. There, he was made to run the gantlet but Logan instructed him how to manage so that he got through without harm. Robinson was then tied to the stake and the Indians prepared to burn him. It was the summer after the murder of Logan's kindred and they had already whipped one Virginian to death merely because his brother was present at the massacre. They could not forgive but Logan rose before the council and pleaded with all his eloquence for Robinson's life. Three times the captive was untied from the stake and three times tied to it again before Logan's words prevailed. At last the great chief was allowed to lay the belt of wampum on the prisoner for a sign that he was adopted. Then he gave him in charge to a young Indian, saying, "This is your cousin; you are to go home with him, and he will take care of you."

But still the sense of his wrong and the hunger for revenge, gnawed at Logan's heart and one day he came to Robinson with a piece of paper and bade him write a letter for him. He said he meant to leave it in the cabin of a white man which he was going to attack and it was afterwards found there tied to a war club. He made Robinson write it several times before he thought the words strong enough. It was addressed to the man whom Logan thought guilty of the death of his kindred but who was afterwards known to have been not even present at their murder:

"Captain Cresap: What did you kill my people on Yellow Creek for? The white people killed my kin at Conestoga, a great while ago, and I thought nothing of that. But you killed my kin again on Yellow Creek, and took my cousin prisoner. Then I thought I must kill, too. I have been three times to war since then; but the Indians are not angry; only myself.

"July 21, 1774.
"Captain John Logan."

Both the matter and the language of this letter are so like those of Logan's famous speech that it is clear he must often have thought his wrongs over in the same terms, brooding upon them with an aching heart but not with hate so much as grief. The speech was made at the Chillicothe town where Lord Dunmore treated with the Ohio tribes for peace in the August after Logan had written his letter but it was not spoken in the council. Logan held aloof from the council and Dunmore sent to his cabin for him. It is said by some that his messenger was the great renegade Simon Girty who had not yet turned against his own people, and was then with his friend Simon Kenton, a scout in Dunmore's service. Others say that the messenger was a young man named Gibson, but whoever he was, Logan met him at the door and coming out into the woods sat down under a tree which was long known as Logan's Elm. Here, with a burst of tears, he told the story of his wrongs in language which cannot be forgotten as long as men have hearts to thrill for others' sorrows.

"I appeal to any white man to say if ever he entered Logan's cabin and I gave him not meat; if ever he came cold and naked and I gave him not clothing. During the course of the last long and bloody war Logan remained in his tent an advocate of peace. Nay, such was my love for the whites that those of my own country pointed at me as they passed, and said, 'Logan is the friend of the white man.' I had even thought to live with you but for the injuries of one man, Colonel Cresap, the last spring, in cold blood and unprovoked, cut off all the relatives of Logan, not sparing even my women and children. There runs not a drop of my blood in the veins of any human creature. This called on me for revenge. I have sought it. I have killed many. I have fully glutted my vengeance. For my country I rejoice at the beams of peace. Yet do not harbor the thought that mine is the joy of fear. Logan never felt fear. He will not turn on his heel to save his life. Who is there to mourn for Logan? Not one."

This speech, or rather this message, which Logan sent to Lord Dunmore has come down to us in two forms, one which Dunmore's officers wrote out from the report of the message and one which Thomas Jefferson framed upon it. They do not differ greatly and I have given Jefferson's version here because it best expresses the noble mind of a noble man, a savage indeed, but far less savage than many of the white men of that day or any day. A pioneer of Western Pennsylvania, William Brown, who afterwards became a judge of the Mifflin County courts, calls him "the best specimen of humanity he ever met with, *white* or red." He first saw him in the woods, while stooping to drink at a spring. The figure of a tall Indian showed itself to him in the water and he sprang for his rifle but the Indian knocked the priming out of his own gun and offered his hand. It was Logan and he guided Brown to the hunting camp of another white man with whom he afterwards visited Logan's camp. There they all shot at a mark for a dollar each round, and Logan lost. A deerskin was worth a dollar and Logan offered five skins for his five failures. Brown's friend refused them saying they were his guests and had shot with him merely for a trial of skill. Logan answered with dignity, "Me try to make you shoot your best; me gentlemen, and me take your dollar if me beat," and he would not allow the victor even to give him a horn of powder in return.

A lovely story was told by the daughter of Judge Brown concerning Logan, who was one day at her father's camp when her mother happened to regret that she had no shoes for her little one then just beginning to walk. Logan said nothing but shortly after he came and asked the mother to let the child spend the day with him at his camp.

The mother trembled but she knew the delicacy of Logan and she would not wound him by showing fear of him. He took the child away and the long hours passed till nightfall. Then she saw the great chief coming with his tiny guest through the woods and the next moment the child bounded into the mother's arms, proud and glad to show her feet in the moccasins which Logan had made for her.

In his old age Logan wandered from place to place, broken by the misfortunes of his people, and homeless in his own land. He fell a prey to drink, the enemy of all his race and he was at last murdered near Detroit, where, as the story goes, he was sitting by his camp fire with his blanket over his head and lost in gloomy thought, when an Indian whom he had offended stole upon him and sank his tomahawk in Logan's skull.

Of all the Indians he seems to me the grandest because he was the kindest. Tecaughretanego was wise and good. He had a thoughtful mind and a serene spirit; he could be just and loving to the white man whom he had taken for his brother, but he had not so noble an ideal of conduct as Logan. This chief grasped the notion of friendship with all the whites; he was more than a tribesman; he imagined what it was to be a citizen. Among the Ohio men of the past there is no nature more beautiful, no memory worthier than his. He was a savage and his thirst for vengeance, or rather the smoldering thought of his wrongs, lowered him for a time to the level of the white and red men about him. Yet he was framed for gentleness and he surpassed another great Ohio Indian as much in breadth of character as he surpassed Tecaughretanego in an ideal of conduct.

Tecumseh, the famous war chief of the Shawnees, was born at the ancient town of Piqua on Mad River, not far from the present city of Springfield in Clark County. His name means Shooting Star and he was indeed the meteoric light of his people while he lived. He was of a high Indian family of the Turtle Tribe and his father had come with his clan to Ohio from their home in Florida about the middle of the last century. Tecumseh was born, as nearly as can be reckoned, in the year 1768 and from his earliest childhood he showed the passion for war which ruled him through life. He led his playmates in their mimic fights and at seventeen he went on his first war party against the Kentuckians. The Indians attacked some boats on the Ohio River and killed all the boatmen but one, whom they brought back and burned at the stake. Tecumseh was present and though he said nothing, the sight of the torture filled him with such horror, that he used his power with the Indians to put a stop forever to the burning of prisoners. He was such a hater of our race that, as he once confessed, the mere presence of a white man made the flesh of his face creep. But he hated cruelty more and in the bloody events which he spent all his power in bringing about, he could always be trusted to keep the captives from torture and to save the lives of women and children.

In spite of his hatred of white men, it is said that he was once in love with a white woman, the daughter of a settler in Greene County. He offered her fifty silver brooches if she would marry him but she refused, saying that she did not wish to be a wild woman and drudge like a squaw; and she would not be tempted even when he promised her that she should not work, but should be a great squaw.

He was not always terrible, even with white men, and it is told of him that once meeting in a settler's cabin a stranger who showed alarm at sight of him, Tecumseh went up and amiably shook him, saying, "Big baby, big baby." But he could be fierce and arrogant when he chose, and he delighted to make the Americans bend to him. At one of their parleys General Harrison asked him to sit on his veranda with him. Tecumseh haughtily refused and forced the general to come out and meet him under the trees, on the breast of the earth who was, he said, the Indian's mother.

He was in every fight with the Americans before Wayne's victory but he was not made a chief until the year following that battle. Then, though he seemed resigned to the fate of his people, he became the leader in their discontent and in the parts of Ohio and Indiana where he lived he kept it alive. In this he had the help of his brother Tenskwatawa, the Prophet, who pretended to have dreams and revelations favorable to Tecumseh's designs. In 1806, while they were Greenville, the Prophet somehow learned that there was to be an eclipse of the sun; he foretold the coming miracle, and excited the savages through their superstitions so dangerously that Governor Harrison urged them to banish the Prophet. They made evasive answers, and kept the Prophet with them, while Tecumseh amused the governor with meetings and parleys, and went and came upon his errands among the Southern tribes stirring them up to join the Northern nations in a revolt against the Americans.

He used all his eloquence and reason in trying to form this union of the red men, and when these would not avail, he did not scruple to employ the arts of his brother. In exhorting one of the Southern tribes he rebuked their coldness and told them that when he reached Detroit, he would stamp his foot and they should feel the earth tremble as a sign of his divine authority for his work. About the time it would have taken him to reach Detroit, the great earthquake of 1810* shook the Seminoles with terror of the man whose arguments they had rejected.

*This earthquake was centered in the New Madrid fault in southeastern Missouri. It actually occurred December 16th, 1811 with aftershocks through February 17th 1812.

In fact, Tecumseh and the Prophet constantly played into each other's hands, but in one of Tecumseh's absences the Prophet made the mistake of attacking General Harrison at Tippecanoe and the savages were severely beaten. The Prophet had also made the mistake of promising them a victory and after the defeat he lost his power over them.

This was in 1811, but the next year the war between the United States and Great Britain broke out and then Tecumseh seized his chance for renewing the war against the Americans. He served so faithfully against them that the king made him Brigadier General and Tecumseh tried to fight according to the laws of civilized warfare. At the attack on Fort Meigs in Wood County he stopped, at the risk of his own life, the massacre of the American prisoners and he bade the British commandant, who declared that the Indians could not be controlled, go and put on petticoats. An American who saw him at this time says, "This celebrated chief was a noble, dignified personage. His face was finely proportioned, his nose inclined to be aquiline and his eye displayed none of that savage and ferocious triumph common to the other Indians on that occasion."

Tecumseh with his Indians witnessed the battle of Lake Erie at Put-in-Bay where Perry defeated the English fleet and he was not deceived by the pretense of General Proctor that the Americans were beaten and the English ships were merely putting in there for repairs. Proctor was then preparing to retreat into Canada from Detroit and Tecumseh demanded to be heard in the name of the Indians. He had some very bitter words to say: "The war before this our British father gave the hatchet to his red children. In that war our father was thrown upon his back by the Americans and our father took them by the hand without our knowledge and we are afraid our father will do so again at this time. Our ships have gone away and we are much astonished to see our father tying up everything and preparing to run away. We are sorry to see our father doing so without seeing the enemy. We must compare our father's conduct to a fat dog that carries his tail on his back and when affrighted drops it between his legs and runs off. Father, you have got the arms and ammunition which our great father sent for his children. If you have an idea of going away, give them to us, and you may go and welcome. Our lives are in the hands of the Great Spirit. We are determined to defend our lands and if it be his will, we wish to leave our bones upon them."

But the British retreated, and the Indians had to follow them into Canada. There in the Battle of the Thames, the Americans defeated them and their savage allies with great slaughter and Tecumseh, whose war cry had been heard above the tumult of the onset, was among the slain. He is supposed to have been killed by a pistol shot fired by Colonel Richard M. Johnson of Kentucky and it is said that the body of this generous enemy did not escape barbarous usage at the hands of

Johnson's men, who literally flayed it and bore portions of their ghastly trophy home with them in triumph.*

*Simon Kenton, present at the battle and who knew Tecumseh personally, said that it was not Tecumseh that the men butchered but another Indian they thought was Tecumseh. The Shawnee later retrieved the body of their fallen leader and removed it from the field.

Tecumseh played, at a later day, the part which Pontiac attempted at the end of the old French War. He tried to unite the Indians in a general uprising against the Americans as Pontiac had united them against the English. He used the same arts and he showed himself shrewd and skillful in paltering with our leaders till he was ready to strike his blow against them, for he managed to remain in the Ohio country unmolested while he was getting ready to drive the Americans out of it. When the war with Great Britain began, he might very well have believed that his hopes were about to be fulfilled. But he seems, though a brave warrior, never to have shown such generalship as that of Little Turtle at St. Clair's defeat. He was a great orator of such a fiery eloquence that the interpreters often declared it impossible for them to give the full sense of his words; but none of his many recorded speeches have the pathos of Logan's. He was, on the savage lines, a statesman and a patriot but unlike the wiser and gentler Logan, he never could rise to the wisdom of living in peace with the whites. He was always an Indian; even at his best he was a savage, just as the backwoodsman was a savage at his worst. Yet his memory remains honored in tradition beyond that of any other Ohio Indian and his name was given to one of the most heroic Ohio Americans, William Tecumseh Sherman. Such as he was and such as Logan was, it must be owned that they seem now of a far nobler mold than any white men in early Ohio history.

The Prophet outlived his brother many years and died dishonored and stripped of all the great power he had once wielded. At one time he wrought so strongly upon the Indians through their superstition of witchcraft, that they put many to death at his accusal. One of the victims was the Wyandot Chief Leatherlips whom six Wyandot warriors came from Tippecanoe to try where he lived near the site of Columbus. They found him guilty and sentenced him to death, of course upon no evidence. A white man who wished to save him asked what he had done, and was answered, "Very bad Indian; make good Indian sick; make horse sick; make die; very bad chief."

When he heard his sentence, Leatherlips ate a hearty dinner, dressed himself in his finest clothes, painted his face, and at the hour fixed for his death walked from his lodge to his grave, chanting his death song while he went. Then as he knelt in prayer beside the shallow pit, one of the six Wyandots tomahawked him.

The persecutions for witchcraft under the Prophet continued until at last a young warrior, whose sister was accused in the council, had the courage to rise and lead her out of the house. He came back and said to the council, pointing at the Prophet, "The devil has come amongst us, and we are killing each other." This bold good sense brought the Indians to a pause in a frenzy which has raged among every people in times past.

Chapter Sixteen
Life in the Backwoods

AMIDST all this tomahawking and scalping, this shooting and stabbing, this shedding of blood and of tears, this heartbreak of captivity, this torture, this peril by day and by night, the flower of home was springing up wherever the ax let the sun into the woods. It would be a great pity if the stories of cruelty and suffering which seem, while we read them, to form the whole history of the Ohio country, should be left without the relief of facts quite as true as these sad tales.

Life was hard in those days, but it was sweet too, and it was often gay and glad. In times of constant danger and even while the merciless savages were beleaguering the lonely clusters of cabins, there was frolicking among the young people in the forts and the old people looked on at their joys in sympathy as well as wonder. The savages themselves had their harmless pleasures and their wild life was so free that those who once knew it did not willingly forsake it. They were not bad-hearted so much as wrong-headed, and they were mostly what they were because they knew no better. More than once we read how the lurking hunter heard them joking and laughing when off their guard in the wood. And in their towns, on the Miamis or the Muskingum or the Sandusky, they had their own games and feasts and merrymakings. Much that was beautiful and kindly and noble was possible to them, but they belonged to the past, and the white men belonged to the future; and the war between the two races had to be. Our race had outgrown the order which theirs clung to helplessly as well as willfully and it was fated that we must found our homes upon their graves.

These homes were at first of the rude and simple sort which a thousand narratives and legends have made familiar and which every Ohio boy and girl has heard of. It would not be easy to say where or when the first log cabin was built but it is safe to say that it was somewhere in the English colonies of North America. And it is certain that it became the type of the settler's house throughout the whole Middle-West. It may be called the American house, the Western house, the Ohio house. Hardly any other house was built for a hundred years by the men who were clearing the land for the stately mansions of our day. As long as the primeval forests stood, the log cabin remained the woodsman's home. And not fifty years ago, I saw log cabins newly built in one of the richest and most prosperous regions of Ohio. They were, to be sure, log cabins of a finer pattern than the first settler reared. They were of logs handsomely shaped with the broadax; the joints between the logs were plastered with mortar; the chimney at the end was of stone; the roof was shingled, the windows were of glass and the door was solid and well hung. They were such cabins as the Christian Indians dwelt in at Gnadenhutten and such as were the homes of the well-to-do settlers in all the older parts of the West. But throughout that region there were many log cabins, mostly sunk to the uses of stables and corn cribs, of the kind that the borderers built in the times of the Indian Wars from 1750 to 1800. They were framed of the round logs, untouched by the ax except for the notches at the ends where they were fitted into one another. The chimney was of small sticks stuck together with mud and was as frail as a barn swallow's nest. The walls were stuffed with moss, plastered with clay, the floor was of rough boards called puncheons, riven from the block with a heavy knife. The roof was of clapboards split from logs and laid loosely on the rafters and held in place with logs fastened athwart them.

There is a delightful account of such a log cabin by John S. Williams, whose father settled in the woods of Belmont County in 1800. "Our cabin," he says, "had been raised, covered, part of the cracks chinked, and part of the floor laid, when we moved in on Christmas day. There had not been a stick cut except in building the cabin which was so high from the ground that a bear, wolf, panther, or any animal less in size than a cow could enter without even a squeeze. The green ash puncheons had shrunk so as to leave cracks in the floor and doors from one to two inches wide. At both the doors we had high, unsteady and sometimes icy steps made by piling the logs cut out of the walls. For the doors and the window, if it could be called a window, when perhaps it was the largest spot in the top, bottom, or sides of the cabin where the wind could *not* enter. It was made by sawing out a log and placing sticks across and then by pasting an old newspaper over the hole and applying hog's lard. We had a kind of glazing which shed a most beautiful and mellow light across the cabin when the sun shone on it. All other light entered at the doors, cracks and chimneys. Our cabin was twenty-four by eighteen. The west end was occupied by two beds, the center of each side by a door. On the opposite side of the window, made of clapboards, supported on pins driven into the walls, were our shelves. On these shelves my sister displayed in simple order, a host of pewter plates and dishes and spoons, scoured and bright. Our chimney occupied most of the east end with pots and kettles opposite the window, under the shelves, a gun on hooks over the north door, four split-bottomed chairs, three three-legged stools and a small eight by ten looking glass sloped from the wall over a large towel and comb case. We got a roof laid over head as soon as possible but it was laid of loose clapboards split from a red-oak, and a cat might have shaken every board in our ceiling. We made two kinds of furniture. One kind was of hickory bark with the outside shaved off. This we would take off all around the tree, the size of which would determine the caliber of our box. Into one end we would place a flat piece of bark or puncheon, cut round to fit in the bark, which stood on end the same as when on the tree. A much finer article was made of slippery-elm bark, shaved smooth, with the inside out, bent round and sewed together where the end of the hoop or main bark lapped over. This was the finest furniture in a lady's dressing room," and such a cabin and its appointments were splendor and luxury beside those of the very earliest pioneers, and many of the latest.

The Williamses were Quakers and the mother was recently from England. They were of far gentler breeding and finer tastes than most of their neighbors who had been backwoodsmen for generations.

When the first settlers broke the silence of the woods with the stroke of their axes and hewed out a space for their cabins and their fields, they enclosed their homes with a high stockade of logs for defense against the Indians; or if they built their cabins outside the wooden walls of their stronghold, they always expected to flee to it at the first alarm and to stand siege within it. The Indians had no cannon and the logs of the stockade were proof against their rifles. If a breach was made, there was still the blockhouse left, the citadel of every little fort. This was heavily built and pierced with loopholes for the riflemen within, whose wives ran bullets for them at its mighty hearth and who kept the savage foe from its sides by firing down upon them through the projecting timbers of its upper story. But in many a fearful siege the Indians set the roof ablaze with arrows wrapped in burning tow and then the fight became desperate indeed. After the Indian War ended, the stockade was no longer needed and the settlers had only the wild beasts to contend with and those constant enemies of the poor in all ages and conditions — hunger and cold.

Winter after winter, the Williamses heard the wolves howling round them in the woods and this music was familiar to the ears of all the Ohio pioneers who trusted their rifles for both the safety and support of their families. They deadened the trees around them by girdling them with the ax and planted the spaces between the leafless trunks with corn and beans and pumpkins. These were their necessaries, but they had an occasional luxury in the wild honey from the hollow of a bee tree when the bears had not got at it. In its season, there was an abundance of wild fruit, plums and cherries, haws and grapes, berries and nuts of every kind and the maples yielded all the sugar they chose to make from them. But it was long before they had, at any time, the profusion which our modern arts enable us to enjoy the whole year round and in the hard beginnings the orchard and the garden were forgotten for the fields. Their harvests must pay for the acres bought of the government or from some speculator who had never seen the land. And the settler must be prompt in paying or else see his home pass from him after all his toil into the hands of strangers. He worked hard and he fared hard, and if he was safer when peace came, it is doubtful if he were otherwise more fortunate. As the game grew scarcer, it was no longer so easy to provide food for his family. The change from venison and wild turkey to the pork, which early began to prevail in his diet, was hardly a wholesome one. Besides, in cutting down the trees, he opened spaces to the sun which had been harmless enough in the shadow of the woods but which now sent up their ague-breeding miasms. Ague was the scourge of the whole region and it was hard to know whether the pestilence was worse on the rich levels beside the rivers or on the stony hills where the settlers sometimes built to escape it. Fevers of several kinds prevailed and consumption was common in the climates that ague spared. There was little knowledge of the rules of health and little medical skill for those who lost it. Most of the remedies for disease and accident were such only as home nursing and home treatment could supply.

When once the settler was housed against the weather, he had the conditions of a certain rude comfort indoors. If his cabin was not proof against the wind and rain or snow, its vast fireplace formed the means of heating while the forest was an inexhaustible store of fuel. At first he dressed in the skins and pelts of the deer and fox and wolf and his costume could have varied little from that of the red savage about him, for we often read how he mistook Indians for white men at first sight, and how the Indians in their turn mistook white men for their own people. The whole family went barefoot in the summer but in winter the pioneer wore moccasins of buckskin, and buckskin leggins or trousers. His coat was a hunting shirt belted at the waist and fringed where it fell to his knees. It was of homespun, a mixture of wool and flax called linsey-woolsey and out of this the dresses of his wife and daughters were made. The wool was shorn from the sheep, which were so scarce that they were never killed for their flesh, except by the wolves which were very fond of mutton, but had no use for wool. For a wedding dress a cotton check was thought superb and it really cost a dollar a yard. Silks, satins, laces, were unknown. A man never left his house without his rifle. The gun was a part of his dress and in his belt he carried a hunting knife and a hatchet. On his head he wore a cap of squirrel skin, often with the plume-like tail dangling from it.

The furniture of the cabins was, like the clothing of the pioneers, homemade. A bedstead was contrived by stretching poles from forked sticks driven into the ground and laying clapboards across them. The bedclothes were bearskins. Stools, benches, and tables were roughed out with auger and broadax. The puncheon floor was left bare and if the earth formed the floor, no rug ever replaced the grass which was its first carpet. The cabin had but one room where the whole of life went on by day. The father and mother slept there at night and the children mounted to their chamber in the loft by means of a ladder.

The food was what has been already named. The meat was venison, bear, raccoon, wild turkey, wild duck, and pheasant. The drink was water, or rye coffee, or whisky which the little stills everywhere supplied only too abundantly. Wheat bread was long unknown and corn cakes of various makings and bakings supplied its place. The most delicious morsel of all was corn grated while still in the milk and fashioned into round cakes eaten hot from the clapboard before the fire, or from the mysterious depths of the Dutch oven, buried in coals and ashes on the hearth. There was soon a great flow of milk from the kine that multiplied in the pastures in the woods and there was sweetening enough from the maple tree and the bee tree, but salt was very scarce and very dear and long journeys were made through the perilous woods to and from the licks or salt springs which the deer had discovered before the white man or the red man knew them.

The bees which hived their honey in the hollow trees were tame bees gone wild and with the coming of the settlers, some of the wild things increased so much that they became a pest. Such were the crows which literally blackened the fields after the settlers plowed and which the whole family had to fight from the corn when it was planted. Such were the rabbits and such, above all, were the squirrels which overran the farms and devoured every green thing till the people combined in great squirrel hunts and destroyed them by tens of thousands. The larger game had meanwhile disappeared. The buffalo and the elk went first; the deer followed, and the bear, and even the useless wolf. But long after these the poisonous reptiles lingered, the rattlesnake, the moccasin, and the yet deadlier copperhead; and it was only when the whole country was cleared that they ceased to be a very common danger.

For a long time there were no mills to grind the corn, and it was pounded into meal for bread with a heavy wooden pestle in a mortar made by hollowing out some tough-grained log. The first mills were horse power; then small water-power mills were put up on the streams and in the larger rivers boats were anchored with mill wheels which the rapid current turned. But the stills were plentier than the mills and as much corn was made into whisky as into bread. Men drank hard to soften their hard life, to lighten its heaviness, to drown its cares, to heighten its few pleasures. Drink was free and common not only at every shooting match, where men met alone, but at every log rolling or cabin raising where the women met with them, to cook for them, and then to dance away the night that followed the toilsome day.

There were no rich people then, but all were poor together, and there were no classes. They were so helpless without one another that people were kindlier and friendlier as well as freer then than now and they made the most of the corn huskings and quilting bees that brought old and young together in harmless frolics. The greatest frolic of all was a wedding. The guests gathered from twenty miles around, and the frolic did not end with the dancing at night. Next day came the *infair* at the house of the bridegroom and all set off together. When they were within a mile or two, they raced for the bottle which was always waiting for them at the house and the guest whose horse was fleetest, brought it back and made all drink from it, beginning with the bride and groom.

Religion soon tempered the ruder pleasures of the backwoods but the dancing ceased before the drinking. Camp meetings were frolics of a soberer sort, where whole neighborhoods gathered and dwelt in tents for days in the beautiful autumn weather and spent the nights in prayer and song. Little log churches were built at the crossroads and these served the purpose of schoolhouses on week days. But there was more religion than learning in the backwoods and the preacher came before the teacher.

He was often a very rude, unlearned man himself and the teacher was sometimes a rude man, harsh and severe when he was learned. Often he was a Scotch-Irishman whose race gave schoolmasters to the West before New England began to send her lettered legions to the frontier.

Such a teacher was Francis Glass, who was born in Dublin in 1790, and came to Ohio in 1817 to teach the children of the backwoods. One of these afterwards remembered a log-cabin schoolhouse where Glass taught in the twilight let through the windows of oiled paper. The seats were of hewn blocks, so heavy that the boys could not upset them. In the midst was a great stove and against the wall stood the teacher's desk of un-planed plank. But as Glass used to say to his pupils, "The temple of the Delphian god was originally a laurel hut and the muses deign to dwell accordingly in very rustic abodes." His labors in the school were not suffered to keep him from higher aims. He wrote a life of Washington in Latin, which was used for a time as a text-book in the Ohio schools.

In the early days all books were costly and they were even fewer than they were costly; but those who longed for them got them somehow and many a boy who studied them by the cabin fire became afterwards a great statesman, a great lawyer, or a great preacher. In fact, almost every distinguished Ohioan of the past generations seems to have begun life in a log cabin and to have found his way out of the dark of ignorance by the light of its great hearth fire. Their stories are such as kindle the fancy and touch the heart, but now they are tales that are told.

Among the stories of life in the backwoods none are more affecting than those of lost children. In the forests which hemmed in the homes and fields of the settlers, the little ones often strayed away or in their bewilderment failed to find a path back to the cabin they had left among the stumps of the clearing or the leafless trunks of the deadening. In 1804, two children, Lydia and Matilda Osborn, eleven and seven years old, went to fetch the cows from their pasture a mile from their home in Williamsburg, Clermont County. Lydia, the elder of the sisters, left the younger in a certain spot while she tried to head off the wandering cows. It is supposed that she failed, and came back to get Matilda. Then it is supposed that, after searching for her, Lydia gave up in despair and started homeward but found that she no longer knew the way. In the meantime the cows had left their pasture and the younger girl had followed the sound of their bells and got safely back to the village. Night came but no Lydia and now the neighborhood turned out and helped the hopeless father to search for the lost child. They carried torches and rang bells and blew horns and fired guns so that she might see and hear and come to them. And before them all, day and night, ran the father calling, "Lydia, Lydia."

Five hundred men, a thousand men at last, joined in the quest and on the fifteenth morning they found in the heart of the woods a tiny hut, such as a child might build, of sticks and moss, with a bed of leaves inside. A path which led from it to a blackberry patch nearby was beaten hard by the little feet of the wanderer. The rough backwoodsmen broke into tears when the father came up and at sight of the poor shelter called out, "Oh, Lydia, Lydia, my dear child, are you yet alive?" They never found her. A mile or two from the hut they found her bonnet and a few miles further on an Indian camp. They could only guess that the Indians had carried her away and go back to their homes without her. The father never gave up, but as long as he lived he searched for her among the Indians. It was thought afterwards that the very means, the lights and the noises, used to attract the child, might have frightened her from her rescuers; for a strange craze would come upon lost people after a time and they would hide from those who were looking for them.

Others became hopelessly bewildered, and it is told of a pioneer, Samuel Davy, who was lost near Galion, that he wandered about till he reached a log cabin in a clearing. There he asked of the woman at the door if she knew where Samuel Davy lived. She laughed and bade him come in and see. Then he knew that it was his own wife speaking to him from his own threshold.

Whenever a lost child could not be found, the Indians were naturally suspected of stealing it; and this was probably the fate of a little one whom her mother lifted over the fence into the dooryard of her cabin near Galion and then went back to her work of making sugar in the woods. When she came home at nightfall, the child was not there and no search afterwards availed to find her, though the whole neighborhood searched the woods for days and nights. It was known only that a party of Indians had lately camped near and that they might have taken the child and brought it up as their own, but the mother never heard of her again.

Galion is rather famous for lost people, but at least one of them was found again. This was a little girl of the name of Bashford who was sent to bring home the cows. In trying to return she became confused and she wisely decided to keep with the cattle. When they lay down for the night, she sheltered herself against the warm back of a motherly old cow and then followed them about in the morning till the neighbors found her.

She was none the worse for the night's adventure except for her fright at the howling of the wolves and from the pain of her slightly frostbitten feet. But the fate of a little boy who wandered from home in Williams County was of a singular pathos. He was found dead after a three-day search, when the poor little body, which was half clad, was still warm. It was supposed that he had undressed each night when he lay down to sleep as he was used to do at home and that the third night he had been so chilled by the October cold that he could not put on all his clothes again, and so strayed feebly about till he lay down and died just before rescue came.

Encounters with wolves and bears were not as common as these animals were, by any means; but now and then the settlers came in conflict with them. In Crawford County so lately as 1826, a young man named Enoch Baker, in coming home from rather a late call on a young lady, fought a running fight with wolves which left him only when he reached the clearing where his father's cabin stood; then they fell back into the woods. Daniel Cloe, a boy of the same neighborhood, was attacked by a pack of eleven wolves one morning before daybreak but was saved by his bulldog which seized the foremost wolf by the throat and gave the boy time to climb a tree.

A brother of this boy found his dogs one morning in ferocious clamor about some animal which they seemed afraid to grapple with. He came up and found that it was a bear. He had no gun but he caught up a club, and when he had contrived to catch the bear by one of his hind legs and to throw him over, he beat him about the head with his bludgeon and killed him.

This was pretty well for a boy of sixteen, but the reader must not award the palm to him without first knowing the adventure of John Gillett of Williams County, who clambered down a hollow tree to get some bear cubs. While he was securing them, the opening overhead was darkened by the body of the mother bear. There was only one thing to do and Gillett drove his knife into the haunch of the bear which scrambled out in surprise and terror and pulled him and the cubs out with her. She did not stay to look after her family and Gillett took the cubs to the next town and got five dollars apiece for them. As he told this story himself, I suppose it must have been true.

There are some stories of wolves and bears in Ashtabula County which are by no means bad. Not the worst of these is told of Elijah Thompson who was hunting in the woods near Geneva when a pack of seven wolves fell upon his dog. He clubbed his rifle and beat them off. Then, when the last had slunk away, he gathered up his wounded dog under his arm and walked away with the barrel, which was all that was left of his rifle, on his shoulder.

Bears were very common, and very fond of pork. One night two ladies, who were alone in their cabin, were alarmed by wild appeals from the pigpen and found it invaded by a bear. They tried to frighten the intruder away with firebrands but failed. Then they loaded the family rifle, which they had heard the men folks say took two fingers of powder. They therefore poured in the powder to the depth of six inches, and drove home the bullet. One held a light while the other pulled the trigger. Both were knocked down by the recoil of the gun which flew into the bushes. What became of the bear was never known, but it was probably blown to atoms.

Other pioneer women were effective with firearms and Mrs. Sarah Thorp of Ashtabula County was one of these. The family fell short of food in their first year in the backwoods and in June, 1799, the husband started to Pennsylvania, twenty miles away, to get supplies. Before he could return, his wife and little girls had begun to live upon roots and the few grains of wheat which she found in the straw of her bed. When these were all gone and she was in despair, a wild turkey one day alighted near the cabin. She found that there was barely powder enough left in the house for the lightest charge; but she loaded her husband's rifle and crept on her hands and knees from bush to bush and log to log till she was close upon the bird, wallowing in the loose plowed earth. Then she fired and killed it and her children were saved.

Starvation was one of the horrors which often threatened the newcomers in the wilderness as it had often beset its improvident red children. In the first year of the settlement at Conneaut, James Kingsbury was forced to leave his family and go some distance into New York state. He fell sick, and was unable to return before winter set in. Then he hurried homeward as fast as he could with a sack of flour on horseback. His horse became disabled and then he carried the flour on his shoulders. He reached home one day at nightfall, and found his older children starving; his wife, wasted with famine, lay on the floor, and near her the little one born in his absence, already dead for want of the nourishment which the poor mother could not give it.

Chapter Seventeen
The First Great Settlements

GENERAL RUFUS PUTNAM, a brave officer of the Revolutionary war, was the first to call the attention of the Eastern States to the rich territory opened to settlement west of the Ohio by the peace with Great Britain and he was one of the earliest band of pioneers which landed on the shores of the Muskingum. In 1787 Rev. Manasseh Cutler of Ipswich, Massachusetts, published a description of the Ohio country which left little to the liveliest imagination. If anything was naturally lacking for the wants of man in a land abounding in wild fruits, "herds of deer, elk, buffalo, and bear," and flocks of "turkeys, geese, ducks, swans, teal, pheasants, partridges, etc., in greater plenty than the tame poultry are in any part of the old settlements of America," and in rivers "stored with fish, especially catfish, the largest, and of a delicious flavor," which " weighs from thirty to eighty pounds," it could be easily supplied by art. "The advantages of every climate," Dr. Cutler told his readers, "are here blended together," and the rich soil, everywhere underlain with valuable minerals and covered with timber waiting to be built into ships and floated down the rivers to the sea, would produce not only "wheat, rye, Indian corn, buckwheat, oats, barley, flax, hemp, tobacco," but even "indigo, silk, wine, and cotton."

It is no wonder that The Ohio Company found the New Englanders eager to come out and possess this goodly heritage and that the first band should have started from Dr. Cutler's own village. At dawn, on the 30th of December, 1787 they paraded before his church and parsonage, twenty-two men with their families. After listening to a short speech from him they fired a salute and set off, as the lettering on their leading wagon made known, "For the Ohio Country."

It was eight weeks before they reached the headwaters of the Beautiful River, and began to build boats to float down its current to the mouth of the Muskingum. In the meantime, on the 1st of January, 1788, another company left Hartford, Connecticut and in four weeks joined the first. They could not embark on their voyage together until April 2nd, but in five days they arrived at Fort Harmar, beside the Muskingum, and were at their journey's end. They did not find the shores waving with indigo, silk, and cotton, but they saw that the soil could produce almost any crop and the weather was so mild and lovely that they must have been confirmed in their belief of all that Dr. Cutler had told them of the climate. Captain Pipe, the Delaware chief who had brought Crawford to his death of cruel torment a few years before, was encamped for trade near the military post and with seventy other Indians he welcomed the newcomers to the Muskingum, where they wisely built a stockade as soon as they could for defense against their red friends. They settled down at once to hew their fields out of the forest and the very next year they had a school for their children. Bathsheba Rouse taught this first Ohio school and Ohio women may well be proud that she taught it a whole year before a man taught the next Ohio school. The settlers called their town Adelphia but soon changed its name to Marietta, which they made up from the name of the French Queen Marie Antoinette, though Marietta was a common enough name in Italian before their invention of it.

They built mills on the streams and in the streams where the current turned their wheels and after a first summer of rejoicing they quieted down to the serious business of clearing farms, having ague, and saving their scalps from the hospitable Delaware and their allies. The very year after their arrival the wonderful climate behaved so ungratefully that the corn crop was cut off by an early frost and something like a famine followed. But still the year of the settlement was one of high hopes and sober jollity. The pioneers celebrated the Fourth of July, 1788 with a grand banquet of "venison barbecued, buffalo steaks, bear meat, wild fowl and a little *pork* as the choicest luxury of all," and at least "one fish, a great pike, weighing one hundred pounds and over six feet long," which could easily be "the largest ever taken by white men in the waters of the Muskingum." Several of the Indians, who were always ready for eating and drinking, took part in the celebration and the settlers saw with pleasure that they did not like the sound of the cannon. They all "kept it up till after twelve o'clock at night and then went home and slept till daylight."

The Marietta people knew how to enjoy themselves, but they had not come to Ohio for pastime and they were soon all hard at work improving themselves as well as their lands. They not only had the first school in Ohio but the first Sunday school. They had a public library in 1796 and preaching in the blockhouse from the beginning. It was ordered that everyone should keep the Sabbath by going to church and all men between eighteen and forty should do four days of military duty every year as well as "entertain emigrants, visit the sick, clothe the naked, feed the hungry, attend funerals, cabin raisings, log rollings, huskings; have their latchstrings always out." Perhaps the reader has heard before this of having the latchstring out but has not known just what the phrase meant. The log cabin door in those days was fastened with a wooden latch on the inside which could be lifted on the outside by a leathern string passed through a small hole in the door above it. When the string was pulled in, the door was locked, but the free-hearted man always left his latchstring out so that every comer could enter and share his fireside with him.

The good people of Marietta had soon occasion for all the kindness enjoined by their laws in befriending a hapless colony of Frenchmenwhom certain speculators known as the Scioto Company had lured from their homes in the Old World and then abandoned to their fate in the heart of the Western wilderness where they had been promised that they were to find "a climate wholesome and delightful, frost even in winter almost entirely unknown, a river called, by way of eminence, the *beautiful* and abounding in excellent fish of a vast size; noble forests consisting of trees that spontaneously produce sugar, and a plant that yields ready-made candles; venison in plenty, the pursuit of which is uninterrupted by wolves, foxes, lions, or tigers; no taxes to pay, no military services to be performed."

Some of the adventurers who came to Ohio on these flattering terms were destitute people who agreed to work three years for the company and were then each to receive from it in reward for their labors fifty acres of land, a house and a cow. But others were people of means who joyfully sold their property in the French cities and came out to found new homes in the Western woods with money in their hands, but with no knowledge of woodcraft, or farming and able neither to hunt, chop, plow, sow, or reap for themselves. They were often artisans, masters of trades utterly useless in that wild country for what were carvers and gilders, cloak makers, wigmakers and hairdressers to do on the banks of the Ohio in 1790? Some ten or twelve peasants came with the rest but they were helpless too in the strange conditions and if it had not been for the settlers at Marietta, they would all have fared miserably indeed.

The Scioto Company had so far provided for them as to agree with the Ohio Company for the erection of a little town or village where Gallipolis now stands, and when the first boats arrived with the strangely assorted company, they found a space cut out of the forest and in the clearing eighty log cabins standing upon four streets fronting the river, with a square enclosed by a high stockade and fortified with blockhouses where they might take shelter from the Indians.

The cabins forming this square were of a better sort than those on the streets and there was one meant to serve for a council chamber where the newcomers promptly began to give balls. They arrived late in October and there was nothing for them to do but to wait for the spring, even if they had known how to farm, and in the meanwhile they had as good a time as they could. They did not yet know that the Scioto Company, which failed to pay the Marietta people for building their village, had no power to give them titles to their land and they hopefully spent their money in hiring American hunters to supply them with game.

They seem to have been rather a light-hearted crew, in spite of their misfortunes and sufferings and they not only amused themselves, but they amused their neighbors by their gay unfitness for the backwoods. If they went to fell a tree, half a dozen of them set to work on it with their axes at once and when they had chopped it all round, they pulled it down with a rope to the great danger of their lives and limbs. When they began to make gardens in the spring they followed the rules laid down in some books on gardening which they had brought with them from France and they planted the seeds of such vegetables as they were used to at home. In a climate where "frost even in winter was almost unknown," the Ohio River froze solidly over the year after they came and the hunters brought in little or none of the promised venison, though certainly not molested in the chase "by tigers, lions, or foxes." The colonists were in danger of starving and many of them were already sick of the fevers bred by the past summer's sun on the swamp lands about them. It was one of their few advantages that the Indians did not trouble them much but after killing one of them in mistake for an American, contented themselves with stealing the Frenchmen's cattle.

When the colonists found that the Scioto Company could not give them titles to the farms they had bought with their money or their toil, they began to stray away from the settlement. Some went down the rivers to New Orleans. Others wandered off elsewhere, perhaps to St. Louis or to the French towns in Indiana and Illinois. And when Congress at last came to their relief with a grant of twenty-four thousand acres, there were left at Gallipolis only ninety-two persons, out of the original five hundred colonists, to profit by the nation's generosity. In 1807 few or none of them remained on the spot where they had fondly hoped to make peaceful and happy homes for themselves and their children. It was a sad ending to a romantic story, the most romantic of all the Ohio stories that I know, but we must not blame those who deceived the colonists (not quite wittingly, it seems) for all their woes and disasters. These were partly owing to themselves. The New Englanders who settled at Marietta did not find eighty comfortable cabins waiting for them and they did not hire hunters to provide their food or begin by giving balls. The able and educated men among the French colonists seem to have cowered under their disasters like the rest and some were incurable dreamers. One of the best of them used afterwards to tell how he was descending the Ohio with two philosophers who believed so firmly in the natural innocence and goodness of men that they invited some Indians aboard their boat and were at once tomahawked. Their skeptical companion shot two of the savages and then jumped into the river where he swam for his life, diving at the flash of their guns, till he got safe to the farther shore.

The Frenchmen at Gallipolis were not the stuff that the founders of great states are made of. But the New Englanders at Marietta were and so were the New Jersey men at Cincinnati, who followed next after them in time. These had even a harder struggle in their beginnings than the people at Marietta for there the emigrants made their settlement under the guns of Fort Harmar, in a region loosely held by the milder Delaware tribe of the Algonquin nation. But the lands between the Great Miami and Little Miami were claimed and held by the fierce Miami and Shawnee and they had been so long the battle ground of the Indians and the Kentuckians that the region was called the Shawnee Slaughter House. The great warpath of the tribes ran through it from the Ohio River to Lake Erie and the first white settlers had to build stations with blockhouses and stockades before they could begin to till the ancient fields where from time to time immemorial the Indians had planted and gathered their harvests of corn. The first settlers arrived from New

Jersey in December, 1788, some eight months after the settlement at Marietta, and in a little more than a year a fort was built at Cincinnati and garrisoned with United States troops. But in 1791 a band of five hundred Indians, led by Simon Girty, attacked Dunlap's Station at Colerain. They were beaten off only after a stubborn fight, though the Americans were armed with the cannon which the savages so much dreaded, and before they raised the siege they burned a white prisoner near the station. This was a surveyor and one of those New Jersey men of education and substance who were the earliest settlers in the Symmes Purchase, as the tract between the two Miamis was called.

John Cleves Symmes, a prominent citizen of Trenton, had bought the land of the government and he came himself with his friends to make the place his home. The events of this emigration were not as poetic as those of the New Englanders who settled on the Muskingum, but they resulted in the foundation of our greatest city, and if the first school in Ohio was at Marietta, the first church was built at Cincinnati. The hamlet opposite the mouth of the Licking was first known as Losantiville, a name made up of Greek and Latin words describing its situation. But this was soon changed to Cincinnati. The fort was built in 1790 and called Fort Washington. It was the strongest fort in the Northwest Territory and to its strength Cincinnati owed her freedom from attacks by the Indians. It was of hewn timber and was eighty feet square. At Cincinnati, Harmar and St. Clair began their march to defeat. Here too the recruits for Wayne's army gathered and encamped before they began their march to victory.

The past of the place is not as rich in legend as that of much humbler localities but there is at least one Indian story which will bear telling over again. It concerns Jacob Wetzel, the brother of the famous Lewis

Wetzel, who was one day returning from a hunt well within the bounds of the present city and had sat down on a log to rest, when a growl from his dog warned him of danger. He instantly *treed,* or jumped behind a tree, and then saw an Indian treed behind a neighboring oak. They both fired; the Indian missed, but Wetzel's bullet had broken the savage's arm. They rushed at each other with their drawn hunting knives and fell in a fearful struggle. Wetzel, unhurt, was no match for the wounded Indian who sat astride of him with his knife lifted when Wetzel's dog sprung at his throat. Wetzel now flung him off and while the dog held him helpless, easily dispatched him.

Another story is of the usual ghastliness relieved by a touch of the comic. Colonel Robert Elliott was shot by the Indians near the northern line of Hamilton County. One of them sprang upon him to scalp him but at a touch the poor man's wig came off in his hand. He lifted it and was heard to say with an oath, "Lie!" while he stared at his trophy in bewilderment.

One of the later captives of the Indians was a boy of eleven named O. M. Spencer who was seized near Cincinnati in 1792 and carried to a Shawnee village on the Maumee where he was taken into a family. His case is peculiarly interesting because Washington himself asked his release through the British Governor of Canada and he was at last returned to his friends by canoe to Detroit, by sailing vessel to Erie, by land to Albany, by water to New York and by land through Pennsylvania to Cincinnati. He was two years in getting back to his friends.

The next settlement in Ohio and the first within the Virginia Military District, was at Massie's Station, now Manchester, where Colonel Nathaniel Massie, with thirty families, arrived in 1790. They at once made themselves safe in an enclosure of strong pickets, fortified with blockhouses and as the woods and rivers abounded in game and fish, they began to lead a life of as much comfort as people could enjoy who were surrounded by a wilderness with the lurking danger of captivity and death on every hand.

Six years later, Colonel Massie laid out the town of Chillicothe, which became the first Capital of Ohio and in the same year, 1796, the earliest settlers from Connecticut landed at Conneaut in Ashtabula County. They were led by Moses Cleaveland, a lawyer of Canterbury, Connecticut, a man of substance and ability. They had come from Buffalo, some by land

and some by water, but they arrived within a few hours of one another. It was the Fourth of July, and Cleaveland wrote in his journal: "We gave three cheers and christened the place Fort Independence; and, after many difficulties, perplexities, and hardships were surmounted and we were on the good and promised land, felt that a just tribute of respect to the day ought to be paid. There were in all, including women and children, fifty in number. The men, under Captain Tinker, ranged themselves on the beach and fired a federal salute of fifteen rounds and then the sixteenth in honor of New Connecticut. Drank several toasts. . . Closed with three cheers. Drank several pails of grog. Supped and retired in good order."

This was the order of the four lawful settlements in the Ohio country: first that of the Massachusetts men at Marietta in July, 1788; next, that of the New Jersey men at Cincinnati in December, 1788; then that of the Virginia men at Manchester in 1790; and then that of the Connecticut men at Conneaut in 1796.

Chapter Eighteen
The State of Ohio in the War of 1812

WE may now begin to speak of the State of Ohio for with the opening of the present century her borders were denned. The rest of the Northwest Territory was called Indiana Territory and by 1804, Ohio found herself a state of the Union. There has never since been any doubt of her being there, and if it had not been for the great Ohio generals there might now be no Union for any of the states to be in. But it is nevertheless true that Ohio was never admitted to the Union by act of Congress and her life as a state dates only from the adoption of her final constitution or from the meeting of her first legislature at Chillicothe on the 1st of March, 1803.

The most memorable fact concerning the adoption of this constitution was the great danger there was that it might allow some form of slavery in the new state. Slavery had been forbidden from the beginning in the Northwest Territory but many of the settlers of the Ohio country were from the slave states of New Jersey, Virginia, Maryland, and Kentucky and there was a strong feeling in favor of allowing women to be held as slaves till they were thirty-five and men till they were twenty-eight years old. But in the end, thanks to one of the Massachusetts men of Marietta, Judge Ephraim Cutler, the friends of slavery were beaten and it was forbidden in Ohio in the same words which had forbidden it in the Northwest Territory.

It had been a long fight and a narrow chance and the clause that gave the future to freedom was carried by one vote only. Edward Tiffin was chosen governor and the new state entered upon a career of peace and comfort if not of great prosperity or rapid progress. The Indians if not crushed were quelled, and the settlers at last lived without fear of them until Tecumseh began his intrigues. In the mean time there was plenty to eat and enough to wear for all. There was the shelter of the log cabin and the fire of its generous hearth. The towns grew, if they did not grow very rapidly; new towns were founded and the country gradually filled up with settlers, or at least the land was claimed. Immense crops were raised on the fertile soil and these were mainly fed to hogs and cattle which more rapidly found a way to market than the grain. They could be driven over the bad roads and the grain had to be carried.

The very richness of the soil when turned to mud forbade good roads in the new country and the most thriving settlements were on the rivers which, as in the days of the Mound Builders, formed the natural highways. Many streams were navigable then which the clearing of the woods from their banks has since turned to shallow pools in the time of drought and to raging torrents in the time of rain; and one of the most hopeful industries was ship building. The trees turned to masts where they grew and many a stately vessel slid into the waters that had washed its living fibers and glided down the Ohio into the Mississippi to the sea.

The Ohio people toiled and waited for the inventions of the future to open ways out into the world for them with the great riches to which they were shut up in their own borders; but it must have been with a growing uneasiness. Great Britain, as we know, had long held the forts in the West which she had agreed to give up to the United States and after she surrendered them, her agents and subjects in Canada abetted the Indians in their rising against the Americans under Tecumseh and the Prophet. The trouble with the Indians would probably have ended at Tippecanoe if it had not been for the outbreak of war between the two countries. Yet this outbreak must have been a kind of relief to the Ohio people. The English insisted upon the right of searching our vessels on the high seas and pressing into their navy any sailors whom they decided to be British subjects and though the Ohio people could not feel the injury of this, as it was felt in the seaboard states whose citizens were forced into the English service by thousands, they could feel the insult. They were used to fighting and they welcomed the war which at least unmasked their enemies. Their ardor was chilled, however, by one of its first events, which was the surrender of Detroit by General Hull. This threw the state open to invasion by the British and Indians and the danger was felt in every part of it. The militia were called out, troops poured in from Kentucky and General Harrison marched into the northwest to recapture Detroit. A detachment of his army was beaten in the first action, which took place beyond the Ohio limits, and after yielding to the British was butchered in cold blood by their Indian allies. The next spring Harrison built Fort Meigs on the Maumee. From this point he hoped to strike a severe blow at the enemy in Canada but he was himself attacked here by General Proctor who marched down from

Maiden with a large force of British regulars, Canadian militia, and Indians led by Tecumseh.

Proctor planted batteries on the shore of the river and Tecumseh's Indians climbed trees and poured down a galling fire on the besieged. The British commander then summoned the fort to surrender, but Harrison answered his messenger, "As General Proctor did not send me a summons on his first arrival, I had supposed that he believed me determined to do my duty," and he dismissed the envoy with the assurance that if the post fell into Proctor's hands it would be in a manner to do him more honor than any surrender could do. The fight then continued until the British General found his fickle savage friends deserting him and on the 12th day raised the siege.

It is probable that the Indians were following their old custom of leaving off fighting to enjoy a sense of victory when they had won it. A large body of Kentucky Horse had, by Harrison's orders, attacked one of the British positions and carried it. After spiking the enemy's guns they pursued the flying British and suddenly fell into an ambush by Indians. Out of eight hundred only one hundred escaped and the work of murdering the prisoners at once began. It was on this occasion that Tecumseh tried to save the lives of the helpless Americans, appealing to the British General to support him and even tomahawking with his own hatchet a disobedient chief who would not give up the work of death.

The allies (British and Indian) made a second attempt on Fort Meigs but they were foiled in this too and then they turned their attention to Fort Sandusky where the town of Fremont now stands. General Harrison held a council of war, and it was decided that Fort Sandusky could not resist an attack and must be abandoned. But when the order to retire reached the gallant young officer in command it was too late, for the Indians were already in force around the post. Major Croghan therefore wrote a reply which he thought might fall into the enemy's hands, and which he worded for their eyes rather than his general's:

"Sir, I have just received yours of yesterday, 10 o'clock p.m., ordering me to destroy this place and make good my retreat, which was received too late to be carried into execution. *We have determined to maintain this place, and by heavens we can!*"

This answer got safely through to General Harrison who promptly resented what he thought its presumption and sent to remove Major

Croghan from his command. Croghan went to explain in person and was allowed to return to his post.

The British and Indians appeared in force the next day, July 31st, and on the 2d of August made their first and last assault. Colonel Short of the British regulars led a force of 350 men against the fort and set them the example of leaping into the ditch before it. When the ditch was full, Croghan opened up on them from a masked porthole with a six pounder and raked them from the distance of thirty feet. Colonel Short, who had ordered his men to give the Americans no quarter, fell mortally wounded. He tied his handkerchief to his sword and waved it in prayer for mercy and not in vain. Croghan did all in his power to relieve his disabled foes. He passed buckets of water to them over the pickets, he opened a space under the pickets that those who could might creep through into the fort out of their comrades' fire.

That night the whole force of the enemy retreated in such haste that they left many stores and munitions behind them. They were commanded by General Proctor who had already failed at Fort Meigs against Harrison and who now dreaded an attack from him. None was made but Harrison had the pleasure of writing in his report of the victory won by Major Croghan at Fort Stephenson:

"It will not be among the least of General Proctor's mortifications that he has been baffled by a youth who had just passed his twenty-first year."

A little more than a month after this repulse the British were defeated in the battle of Lake Erie by Commodore Perry at Put-in-Bay. The action itself is by no means the most impressive part of the wonderful story of that great victory. Perry had not only to cope with the British in waters where they had been undisputed masters, but he had to create the means of doing so. He brought ship builders, naval stores, guns and ammunition, as well as sailors for his fleet, four hundred miles through the wilderness of New York to the wilderness at Erie, Pennsylvania and there he hewed out of the forest the stuff which he wrought almost alive into his ships. On the 1st of August he was ready to sail with two large vessels of twenty guns each and seven smaller craft carrying fourteen guns in all. With these he met the enemy's force of six vessels carrying sixty-four guns and on the beautiful sunny morning of the 10th of September the famous fight took place. The Americans at first had the worst of it. The British guns were of longer range and Perry's flag-ship, the *Lawrence,* was so badly disabled that he had to abandon it for the *Niagara.* The *Lawrence* was in fact an unmanageable wreck. Her decks were streaming with blood but nothing broke the awful order of the carnage. The men fell at their guns; if wounded, they were carried below; if killed, they were left where they dropped while others took their places.

Perry hauled down his colors with his own hand and with his flag under his arm was rowed to the *Niagara* through a storm of musketry. Once on board this vessel, he began to change defeat into victory and after a fight lasting more than three hours in all, he could send to General Harrison his memorable dispatch, *"We have met the enemy and they are ours."*

The next day the mournful sequel to this tragedy followed when the crews of both fleets, victors and vanquished, joined in burying their dead on the shore of the bay. The sailors slain in the battle had been already sunken in the lake but now to the sound of the minute guns from the ships, with the sad music of funeral marches, the measured dip of oars, and the flutter of half-masted flags, the last sad rites were paid to the fallen officers. Perhaps the Indians under Tecumseh, who had seen with stupid dismay the great battle of the rival squadrons, witnessed this pathetic spectacle too, before they sullenly withdrew into Canada after Proctor's army. There Harrison pursued them and in his victory on the banks of the Thames, their mighty chieftain fell and their cause perished with him.

Chapter Nineteen
A Foolish Man, a Philosopher and a Fanatic

WHO is Blennerhassett?" asked William Wirt, at the trial of Aaron Burr for treason and many a schoolboy since has echoed the question, as many a schoolboy will hereafter, while impassioned oratory is music to the ear and witchery to the breast. The eloquent lawyer went on to answer himself and painted in glowing colors a character which history sees in a colder light. But though Blennerhassett was not the ideal that Wirt imagined, he was the generous victim of a cold and selfish man's ambition and the ruin of his happy home and gentle hope is none the less pathetic because his own folly was partly to blame for it.

We must go back of the events which we have been following to an earlier date, if we wish to find Harman Blennerhassett dwelling with his beautiful wife on their fairy island in the Ohio. Their earthly paradise lay in the larger stream at the mouth of the Kanawha, not far from the present town of Belpre, and there in the first year of the century, Blennerhassett built a mansion which became the wonder of the West. The West was not then very well able to judge of the magnificence which it celebrated, but there seems no reason to doubt that Blennerhassett's mansion was fine and of a grandeur unexampled in that new country where most men lived in log cabins and where any framed house was a marvel.

He was of English birth but of Irish parentage and to the ardor of his race he added the refinement of an educated taste. He was a Trinity College man and one of his classmates at Dublin was the Irish patriot, Emmet, who afterwards suffered death for his country. But it does not appear that Blennerhassett came to America for political reasons and he seems to have made his home in the West from the impulse of a poetic nature, with the wealth and the leisure to realize the fancies of his dream.

"A shrubbery that Shenstone might have envied," says Wirt, "blooms around him. Music that might have charmed Calypso and her nymphs is his. An extensive library spreads its treasures before him. A philosophical apparatus offers him all the secrets and mysteries of nature. Peace, tranquility, and innocence shed their mingled delights around him. And to crown the enchantment of the scene, a wife, who is said to be lovely even beyond her sex and graced with every accomplishment that can render it irresistible had blessed him with her love."

Whatever may be the facts concerning the home of the Blennerhassetts, the memories of those who knew its mistress bear witness to the truth of these glowing words. They testify that she was not only brilliant, accomplished, exquisite in manner, but good to everyone, kind to the poor, and devoted to her husband and children. She was a faultless housewife as well as a fearless horsewoman and she was strong in body as she was active in mind. "She could leap a five-rail fence, walk ten miles at a stretch, and ride with the boldest dragoon. Robed in scarlet broadcloth with a white beaver hat, on a spirited horse, she might be seen dashing through the dark woods, reminding one of the flight and gay plumage of a tropical bird."

To this home and its inmates came Aaron Burr, as bad, brave, and brilliant a man as ever figured in our public life. He had been a gallant officer in the Revolution, he had been Vice President of the United States, he had come within a vote of being President. But he had killed Alexander Hamilton in the duel which he forced upon him and all his knowledge of the world and men had taught him to worship power and despise virtue. It has not yet been clearly shown what Burr meant or hoped to do and possibly he could not have very well said himself; but it is certain that in a general way he was trying to separate the West from the East and to commit the warlike people of the backwoods to a fine scheme for conquering Mexico from Spain and setting up an imperial throne there for him to sit upon.

He was always willing to sell out his fine scheme to France, to England, to any power that would buy...even to Spain herself and in the mean time he came and went in the West and Southwest and built up a party in his favor, which fell to pieces at the first touch of real adversity. General Wilkinson, of the United States army, who had been plotting and scheming with Burr, arrested him. He was tried for treason and those who had cast their fortunes with him were carried down in his fall. The most picturesque of the sufferers was Blennerhassett, who was one of the most innocent. Burr had found other Ohio people too plodding, as he said, but the Blennerhassetts took him seriously and when Burr, in his repeated visits, tempted the husband and flattered the wife, who was ambitious only for her husband, he easily beguiled them into a belief in his glorious destiny.

Blennerhassett put all his fortune into the venture. He ordered fifteen large boats built for transporting five hundred men down the Mississippi. He contracted for provisioning them and pledged himself for the payments of all kinds of debts. His friends tried to reason with his folly in vain. Governor Tiffin called out a company of militia to prevent his boats from leaving the Muskingum. Blennerhassett heard that he was to be arrested, and fled. A troop of Virginians seized his island, pillaged his house and ruined his grounds and Mrs. Blennerhassett, with her children, embarked amid the ice-floes of the Ohio on a small flatboat and made her way to her husband in Louisiana. Here he was taken, but discharged after a few weeks' imprisonment. They came back to their island but they never lived there again and in 1811 the house was burned. They wandered from place to place and grew poorer and poorer. In 1831 he died at the house of his sister in the island of Guernsey and seven years later his wife ended her days in a New York tenement house.

Another picturesque figure of our early times was one who never meant and never imagined harm to any living creature, man or beast, but gave his simple, humble life to doing good with no thought of his own advantage. Perhaps as the world grows more truly civilized the name of Johnny Appleseed will be honored above that of some heroes of the Ohio country. Like so many of our distinguished men, he was not born in our state, but he came here in his young manhood from his birthplace in Massachusetts and began at once to plant the apple seeds which gave him his nickname. Few knew that his real name was John Chapman, but it did not matter and Johnny Appleseed became his right name if men are rightly named from their works.

Wherever he went he carried a store of apple seeds with him, and when he came to a good clear spot on the bank of a stream, he planted his seeds, fenced the place in, and left them to sprout and grow into trees for the orchards of the neighborhood. He soon had hundreds of these little nurseries throughout Ohio which he returned year after year to watch and tend, and which no one molested. When the trees were large enough, he sold them to the farmers for a trifle...an old coat or an old shirt and when he needed nothing he gave them for nothing. He went barefoot in the warm weather and in winter he wore cast-off shoes. When he could get none and the ways were very rough he protected his feet with rude sandals of his own making. His hats were of his own making too and were usually of pasteboard with a broad brim in front to shield his eyes from the sun; but otherwise he dressed in the second-hand clothing of others, for he thought it wrong to spend upon the vanities of dress. He dwelt close to the heart of nature whose dumb children he would not wound or kill, even poisonous snakes or noxious insects. The Indians knew him and loved him for the goodness of his life and they honored him for the courage with which he bore the pain he never would inflict. He could drive pins into his flesh without wincing. If he got hurt he burned the place and then treated it as a burn. He bore himself in all things, to their thinking, far above other white men.

It was believed that he had come into the backwoods to forget a disappointment in love but there is no proof that he had ever suffered this. What is certain is that he was a man of beautiful qualities of heart and mind, who could at times be divinely eloquent about the work he had chosen to do in this world. He was a believer in the philosophy of Emanuel Swedenborg; he carried books of that doctrine in his bosom, and constantly read them or shared them with those who cared to know it, even to tearing a volume in two. If his belief was true and we are in this world surrounded by spirits, evil or good, which our evil or good behavior invites to be of our company, then this harmless, loving, uncouth, half-crazy man walked daily with the angels of God.

In those early days when the people were poor and ignorant and had little hope of bettering themselves in this world, their thoughts turned much to the other world. The country was often swept by storms of religious excitement. And at the camp-meetings the devout fell in fits and trances or were convulsed with strange throes called the jerks and all sorts of superstitions grew up easily among them. The wildest of these perhaps was that of the Leatherwood God which flourished in Guernsey County about the year 1828. The name of this fanatic or impostor, who was indeed both one and the other, was Joseph C. Dylks and his title was given him because of his claim to be the Supreme Being and because he first appeared to his worshipers on Leatherwood Creek at the town of Salesville. The leatherwood tree which gave this creek its name had a soft and pliable bark which could be easily tied into knots and was used as cordage by the pioneers; and the dwellers on Leatherwood Creek had a faith of much the same easy texture. Yet they were of rather more than the average intelligence and they were so far from bigoted or intolerant that all sects among them worshiped in one sanctuary. A large cabin which they had built in common and which they called the Temple.

Here on a certain night, while they sat listening to one of their preachers, they were thrilled by a loud cry of "Salvation!" followed by a fierce snort like that of a startled horse and they discovered in their midst a stranger of a grave and impressive aspect, who had come no one knew whence or how. When he rose he stood nearly six feet high, and showed himself of a perfect figure with flashing black eyes, a low broad forehead and a fine arched nose. His hair, black and thick, fell in a mass behind his ears over his shoulders. He wore a suit of black broadcloth, a white neck cloth and a yellow beaver hat. His weird snort and his striking presence seem to have been his sole equipment for swaying the faith of the people; though some of the earliest believers saw a heavenly radiance streaming from his countenance at times and when he rode, they beheld above his head a ring of light which hung in the air over the saddle if he dismounted. But he soon began to make converts and he had quickly enough, of the best among those good men and women, to gain the sole use of the Temple.

At first he claimed merely to be the Lord Jesus Christ but he presently announced himself God Almighty, the maker of heaven and earth and his followers readily believed him, though he failed in the simple miracle of making a seamless garment out of a bolt of linsey-woolsey cloth and kept none of his promises to them. He probably found it sufficient to be the Deity and his worshipers, among whom were two ministers, were certainly content. But the unbelievers felt the scandal to be too great. They had Dylks arrested and brought before two justices of the peace, who one after the other decided that there was no law of Ohio which forbade a man to declare himself the Almighty. The wretched creature was acquitted but he was thoroughly frightened. He made his escape from his guards and took to the woods where he was some time in hiding. When he came back to the believers, he had bated nothing of his claim to divinity but he was no longer so bold. He now told them that the New Jerusalem would not come down at Leatherwood Creek, but in the city of Philadelphia and he departed to the scene of his glory.

Three of the believers followed him over the rugged mountains and through the pathless woods, finding food and shelter by hardly less than a miracle, but they did not find the New Jerusalem at their journey's end. Dylks had told them that where they should see the heavenly light the brightest, there they should behold the beginning of the New Jerusalem. But they nowhere saw this light, though they walked the streets of the earthly city night and day. Two of them were substantial farmers and when they had lost all hope and had lost even Dylks himself (for he soon vanished), they pledged their tobacco crops and so got money enough to come home where they lived and died in the full faith that Joseph C. Dylks was God Almighty, though he never did anything to prove it but snort like a startled horse, wear long hair on foot and a halo on horseback, and fail in everything else he attempted. The third of this company of his followers, a young minister of the United Brethren, did not return for some years; then he came, well dressed and looking fat and sleek and preached to the people on Leatherwood Creek the faith in which he had not faltered. He accounted for the disappearance of Dylks from the eyes of his other worshipers in Philadelphia very simply. He had seen him taken up into heaven.

But the people had merely his word for the fact. Dylks never descended to earth again as his apostle promised and the belief in his divinity died out with those who first accepted him.

Chapter Twenty

Ways Out

IN 1893 Jacob S. Coxey, a respectable citizen of Massillon, started a movement in favor of good roads which took the form of a pilgrimage to Washington to petition Congress for its object. Several armies, as they were called, from different parts of the country, met in Massillon and under Mr. Coxey's leadership, set out on a long and toilsome march over the Alleghenies to the capital, living by charity on the way. Many of the soldiers of these armies might well have been idle and worthless persons. There were doubtless others who were sincere and sane in their hope that the representatives of the people might be persuaded to do something for bettering the highways, but the affair was so managed as to meet with nothing but ridicule and in trying to force a hearing from Congress Mr. Coxey and some of his followers were arrested for trespassing on the Capitol grounds and were sentenced to several weeks in jail. This ended the latest crusade for good roads from Ohio, but there is no Ohio idea more fixed than that we ought to have good roads and this was by no means the first time that Ohio men had asked the nation to lend a hand in making them. The first time they succeeded as signally as they failed the last time. But that was very long ago and it may surprise some of my readers to know that we have a National Road* crossing our whole state, which is still the best road in it.

*Present day U.S. Route 40

Almost as soon as the Western people had broken into the backwoods it became their necessity to break out again, to find and to make roads between them and the civilization they had left. The ways of the different emigrations in reaching Ohio were: for the New Englanders, through New York state to Lake Erie and westwardly along the shore of that water; for the Pennsylvanians, through their own state to the headwaters of the Ohio and then down the river and inwardly from it; for the Virginians, Marylanders, and Carolinians, the valley of the Shenandoah and the mountain gaps to Kentucky and so into Southwestern Ohio.

At first the white men came by the *streets,* as the pioneers called the trails that the buffalo and deer had made, but they soon cut traces through the woods and later these traces became wagon roads. Of course they used the rivers wherever they could and traveled by canoe, by flatboat, by keelboat, and by ark; and there grew up on the rivers a wild life which had its adventures and heroes like the Indian warfare.

The most famous of the boatmen was Mike Fink, who drank hard and fought hard and was a miraculous shot with his rifle. He was captain of a keelboat, which was the craft mostly used in ascending the river. The flatboats were broken up and sold as lumber when they had drifted down to their points of destination on the lower rivers, but the keelboat could make a return trip by dint of pushing with a long pole on the shore side and rowing on the other; sometimes even sails were used and then the keelboat sped up stream at the rate of fifty miles instead of twelve miles a day.

But these means of traffic and travel soon ceased to suffice. Then the Ohio people felt the need of getting out with their increasing crops, their multiplying flocks and herds, and they made their need known to the nation, to which they were everywhere akin, and the nation answered through Congress by beginning in 1806, the National Road which was finished by 1838 from Baltimore as far as Indiana. This road first opened the East to Ohio.

Then, in 1811 a steamboat made its appearance on the Beautiful River and after that steam commanded all the Southern and Southwestern waters for us as well as those of the inland seas on the North.

Then, that all these waters might be united, the state began in 1825 to build a system of canals from Cleveland to Portsmouth and from Toledo to Cincinnati. When these canals were completed with their branches, they gave the people some nine hundred miles of navigable waters within their own borders. The main lines were built not by companies for private profit as the railroads have since been built, but by the people for the people and it may be said that the great prosperity of Ohio began with them. Wherever they ran they drained the swamps and made the land not only habitable but beautiful. They were dug by Ohio people and the sixteen millions of dollars that they cost came back into the hands of the men who gladly taxed themselves for the outlay. The towns along their course grew and new towns rose out of the forests and prairies.

The Ohio people had the impulse to this great work from the New York people who had built the Erie Canal from Albany to Buffalo and whose Governor, De Witt Clinton, had urged forward that work. Now, when our whole state was ablaze with joy at the action of the legislature in providing for the work, Governor Clinton was invited to come and first strike the spade into the earth in digging the new canals. He arrived by steamboat at Cleveland where the people received him and his train of distinguished New Yorkers with rejoicings worthy of the great event. He took stage for Newark and on the 4th of July, 1825, when our state had just come of age, in the presence of all the Ohio magnates and dignitaries and a mighty throng of citizens, he lifted a spadeful from the ground on the Licking Summit. Governor Morrow of Ohio lifted the second spadeful and then followed a struggle among the distinguished men as to which should lift the third.

New Yorkers and Ohioans vied in filling a wheelbarrow with successive spadefuls and a happy citizen of Chillicothe had the honor of wheeling it away and dumping it over a bank. He was the captain of a company of militia and the crowd was so great that a squadron of cavalry had to keep a space for the speakers in the midst of their hollow square. Thomas Ewing delivered the oration and men all round him wept for joy.

There were like scenes when the canals were completed. Multitudes gathered to see the water let into the channels which, to their impatience had been so long in digging, and they took hopefully the disappointment of having it sink into the gravelly beds before it could slowly fill the banks, instead of rushing like a flood to their brims. At Dayton, 1829, when the first fleet of three canal boats arrived from Cincinnati, it was greeted with the firing of cannon and the shouts of an immense crowd lining the canal banks. This was as it should be and will be wherever a great work is done for the common good; and it ought never to be forgotten that the canals of Ohio were dug by Ohio men that all Ohio men might freely prosper more and more and not that a few rich men might get richer.

After the National Road, which was our first way out, came the steam navigation of the lake and the river and after that came the railroad, which will be our main reliance for getting back and forth over the state and to and from it till some of the many schemes of travel through the air are realized. We cannot tell how far off the event may be; but in the mean time it is curious, if not very flattering to our Ohio pride, to learn that the first railroad enterprise within our borders was fostered by Michigan. The legislature of that state granted the charter of the Erie and Kalamazoo Railroad which opened in 1836. The line ran from Toledo to Adrian, thirty-three miles, but when it was projected the matter was so far from serious with the legislature which authorized it that it was granted because it was "merely a fanciful scheme that could do no harm, and would greatly please" certain citizens of Toledo; just as now a balloon line might be laughingly authorized. It was entirely successful, however, as far as the running was concerned, though the road was so hampered by the cost of fighting enemies and the expenses of building that it was seized for debt seven years later.

This has been the history of many railroads since in Ohio, and if we could read between the lines that now cobweb the map of the state, we should come to know many tales of broken fortunes and of broken hopes. The railroads are no different in this from other business enterprises but they are different from the canals. These, as we have seen, were the work of the state for the advantage of the whole people while the railroads were, from the beginning, private schemes for making money.

Each kind of highway came in its time and each in its way served the purpose of Ohio. At the time the companies began to build their railroads, the state system of canals was in its highest usefulness and it is no wonder that the people should have regarded the railroads as fanciful schemes. No one could then have dreamed how rapidly they would increase and multiply and that in less than fifty years they should so far surpass the canals in service to the public that some of these would be abandoned by the state and become grass-grown ditches hardly distinguishable in their look of ancient ruin from the works of the Mound Builders. At the most there were once nine hundred miles of canals in Ohio and now there are twelve or fourteen thousand miles of railroads. Yet the canals were a greater achievement for Ohio in 1837 than the railroads are in 1897.

The children of this day can hardly imagine what rude and simple affairs the earliest railroads were. Instead of the long smooth steel rails which now carry the great trains with their luxurious cars, in their never-ceasing flight, day in and day out the whole year round, flat bands of iron, spiked to wooden rails formed the path of the small carriages drawn by a locomotive of the size and shape of a threshing-machine engine. These amazed by a speed of ten or twelve miles an hour the gaping spectator whose grandchildren do not turn their heads to look at the express as it makes its sixty miles in sixty minutes. In the very beginning, indeed, the carriages were drawn by horses and it was several years before steam was used. Little by little the railroads began to be built on the easy levels of the state and before a great while a line was projected from Cincinnati to Columbus along the course of the Little Miami River. This was completed piecemeal, from point to point, and at last carried through. In the meantime other lines were laid out and then all at once the railroad era was at hand. It was a time of great excitement and expectation, if not of that public rejoicing which had welcomed the canals.

In a few years the magnificent fleets of the river began to feel the fatal rivalry of the trains that swept along its borders. Travel deserted them and traffic sought the surer and swifter transportation of the shore. The great packets that had carried swarms of passengers to and from Pittsburg and Cincinnati and all the points between, disappeared or were converted into freight-boats and then these began to fail for want of traffic, and the Beautiful River was almost abandoned to the stern-wheeler pushing a flotilla of coal-barges. A like change took place upon the lake. Steamers which formed the means of communication between the towns and cities from Cleveland to Buffalo and from Cleveland to Detroit, ceased to touch at the smaller ports and became the pleasure-craft of the summer tourists or the carriers of heavy freight. And the ports which did not become the feeders of the railroads dwindled to insignificance. But the railroads could not affect the navigation of the lake quite so disastrously as that of the river; the lake in such a rivalry had some such advantage as that of the sea from its mere vastness and from the expanses where the railroads could not follow the steamer in the mere nature of things. The iron horse had his way with the canals though, and these monuments of a former period of enterprise grow more and more like its sepulcher, where he drank them dry, or where he left their slow currents to stagnate unstirred by the keels of the leisurely craft once so jubilantly welcomed to them.

Except for the occasional breaking of an embankment, the history of the canals could hardly be marked by any incidents of exciting interest. It was not so with steamboating and railroading which has each its long tale of disasters such as give times of peace almost as dark a record as those of war. The most tragical of these events took place at the opposite extremities of the state, in Cincinnati and in Ashtabula, and they occurred at the beginning and the end of an interval of nearly forty years.

The rise of steamboating on the Western rivers was perhaps all the more rapid because of the daring and reckless spirit of the Western people, who took almost any risk in order to carry a point in their rivalries or to gain an end of their ambition. It is certain at any rate that the builders and the crews of the popular boats joined in contriving and urging them to a speed that should leave all competitors behind. There was frequent racing between the packets on the Ohio and Mississippi, and the frightful calamities from bursting boilers continued for a long time before public opinion quelled the boyish love of victory which tempted not only the steamboatmen but their passengers too. These joined with the captain in forcing the boat to the top of its speed, at the risk of a swift or agonizing death to all on board; and it was no doubt with their full approval that the master of the beautiful new steamer *Moselle* took the chance that resulted in the loss of more than two hundred lives on the 26th of April, 1838. She had just left her moorings at Cincinnati for her trip to Louisville and had run up to take on a family from a raft a little way above the city. In order that she might show her speed before the crowd on the landing and pass a rival boat in sight of all as she returned, the captain held to the full head of steam with which he had started. Her wheels had scarcely turned after she parted from the raft, when her boilers burst with a roar like thunder. The air was instantly filled with the flying fragments of the wreck and with the bodies and the heads and limbs of men, women, and children. These fell, strewing the shore and dropping into the river where what was left of the *Moselle* sank within fifteen minutes. Cries of anguish, groans and shrieks from the sufferers, followed the awful sound of the explosion. Many of the victims whom the accident had spared were drowned before boats could reach them. The mangled body of the captain was hurled into the street; the pilot was thrown a hundred feet into the air and fell back into the stream.

In 1876, on the evening of December 29, an express train of the Lake Shore Railroad broke through the bridge at Ashtabula and plunged seventy-five feet down into the bed of the creek below. The train was of eleven cars with a hundred and fifty-six passengers on board and the bridge was further strained by the weight of the two massive locomotives which drew it. The night was extremely cold and a blinding snow storm was raging while the freezing wind blew a gale. The wreck at once took fire and the cries of the wounded were now mingled with the agonized prayers of those who saw themselves doomed to death in the blazing ruins which imprisoned them. Nearly everyone on the train was hurt more or less severely; eighty persons perished in the fall or the fire and five died after they were rescued.

There were other paths which the Ohio people had to open before they could reach a yet wider world than any that lay to the east of them or the south of them. Their course to civilization lay not only through the woods and down the rivers and over the mountains, but it ran also through the great realm of books and every log schoolhouse was a station or a junction on it; or rather, as they had things in these days, a milestone or a finger-post.

The great glory and strength of the Ohio people, as I have hinted before, came from their varied origin, They have shown themselves among the first of the Americans, not because they were born in Ohio, but because they were born of the Massachusetts and Connecticut men, the New Yorkers and Pennsylvanians, the New Jersey men and Marylanders, the Virginians and Carolinians and Kentuckians who made Ohio what it was to be by the mixture of their characteristics and qualities here. It is of no use to pretend, however, that it was their virtues alone which got into the Ohio people; their foibles got in too, and their prejudices and their vices.

A traveler in our state, just after it had become a state, believed that we were destined to be more like the people of the North and East than the people of the South, whom he then found in Kentucky at least, much livelier in mind and manner than the Pennsylvanians, fond of public life and society, very hospitable and courteous, but dissipated, restless, and reckless. Our public spirit did not come from our Southern ancestry, but from our New England ancestry. The South gave Ohio perhaps her foremost place in war and politics but her enlightenment in other things was from the North. It was the aristocratic indifference of the South to public schools that for twenty-four years after Ohio became a state kept her from profiting by the magnificent provision of school lands made for her by the whole nation through Congress. It was not until almost a generation after Ohio became a state that she began to have schools partly free and it was still a generation later before the men of New England blood framed the present school law and got it enacted by the legislature. This was in 1853, but in 1825 the first great effort for public schools was made. There was then a party in favor of canals in the legislature and another party in favor of schools and these two parties fought each other a long time. At last they united and together gave the people canals and schools, the two ways out of the wilderness.

Our canals are no longer the great avenues of commerce because the modern needs and means are different from those of former days, but our schools are still the royal roads, the people's roads, to and from the world of letters and arts. Ohio is now second to no other state in her public school system and well-nigh three-quarters of a century ago, when General Lafayette visited Cincinnati in his tour of the Republic which he had helped to found, nothing surprised and charmed him more than the greeting which the children of her public schools gave him. It spoke to him of a refined and graceful life such as he could never have imagined in the young city so lately carven out the forests. And such proofs of the general culture must have done more than all the signs of material prosperity, all the objects of industry so proudly shown him, to make him regard Ohio (to use his own words) as the eighth wonder of the world. Six hundred boys and girls from the public schools met him at sunrise on the morning of his arrival and scattered flowers under his feet and made the air ring with their shouts of "Welcome to Lafayette!"

As for the Indians, who fought so long and so hard here for the graves of their fathers and the homes of their children, they had to find their ways out too. But it would not be easy to say what became of them all, for they went such various ways out of Ohio and out of the world. Some remained in the country which they had lost and in a few cases they tried to take on the likeness of civilized men. But oftener they only took on the vices of civilization. They were the drunkards and the vagrants of their neighborhoods, living by a little work and by the contemptuous charity of the settlers. In them the proud spirit of their race was broken.

They suffered insult and outrage from their conquerors without resisting. A small white man might knock a stalwart Indian down with his fist and the Indian would not attempt to revenge himself. For a while, the settlers feared the lingering red men but they soon learned to despise them and it was seldom that they troubled the whites by theft or violence.

A good many of the tribesmen followed the British into Canada after the War of 1812, where it must be owned to our shame as Americans that they had wiser, kinder, and juster treatment than we gave those who remained with us, and who followed westward from their old hunting grounds in Ohio the buffalo, the elk, the beaver, and the deer. Several nations or parts of nations, were gathered on reservations in Seneca, Lucas, and Wyandot counties where they were given land and taught farming and other trades. Missionaries came to dwell among them and try to make them Christians and many were converted. The Quakers seem to have done the best work in this way for the Indians always trusted and loved the men of peace.

But although their friends could teach the Indians to plow and sow, to build houses and barns, to make tools and mend them, to sing and to pray, and to wear clothes and to lead decent and sober lives, they could not uproot all their old customs and superstitions. The superstition that seemed to last longest was the belief in witchcraft, which was indeed very common among their white neighbors. Nearly all forms of sickness were treated as the effect of witchcraft by the Indians and the afflicted were carried into the woods and left alone with none near them except the medicine man whose business it was to expel the witch.

A suspected witch or wizard might be safely killed by any kinsman of the sufferer and it is said that Indians were known to walk all the way from the Mississippi to the Ohio reservations in order to shoot down persons accused of witchcraft and then return unmolested. In 1828, the Mingo chief Seneca John was put to death by two of his tribesmen as ruthlessly as Leatherlips in 1812. He was accused of having bewitched the chief Comstock, and though he protested, "I loved my brother Comstock better than the green earth I stand upon; I would shed my blood, drop by drop, to bring him back to life," yet he was sentenced to die and Comstock's brothers, Coonstick and Steel, carried out the sentence.

In 1831 the Senecas ceded their lands, forty thousand acres on the Sandusky, to the United States and were removed to the southwest of the Missouri. Each of the other reservations was given up in turn for lands in the Far West and in the early forties I myself, when a boy living in Hamilton, saw the last of the Ohio Indians passing through the town on the three canal boats which carried the small remnant of their nation southward and westward out of the land that was to know them no more forever. It was quite a time. I cannot say how far they had been civilized, and for all I know they may have been tame farmers and mechanics, but in their moccasins and blankets, with their bows and arrows, they looked like wild hunters and Ohio was no longer a good hunting ground. All the larger game had long been killed off or driven away and the smaller game was fast vanishing before the rifle and the shotgun.

As if its destruction by gunners singly was not rapid enough it was the custom in somewhat earlier days for whole neighborhoods to meet together for the wholesale slaughter of the sylvan creatures which still abounded. One of these great hunts took place in Medina County in 1818, when the region was as yet very sparsely settled. The drive, as it was called, was fixed for the 24th of December and at sunrise, six hundred men and boys drew up their far-spreading lines. They were armed with rifles, shotguns, old muskets, pistols, knives, axes, hatchets, bayonets fastened to long poles and whatever other weapons they could lay hands on, to shoot, strike, or stab with, and they began to draw their vast circle together with a hideous uproar of horn, conch shells, and voices. The deer fled inward from all sides; bear and wolf left their coverts in terror; foxes and raccoons joined the panic rout and the air was full of the flight of wild turkeys. Then the slaughter began and before it ended three hundred deer, twenty-one bears and seventeen wolves were killed; of the turkeys and the smaller game no tale was kept.

Later these drives were common in the years whenever game was abundant in any neighborhood. They were called squirrel-hunts, because the squirrel was the unit and larger or smaller game counted so many squirrels, or went to make up the value of a squirrel. I knew of one of these hunts during the late fifties in Northern Ohio, when the wild pigeons were still in such multitude that their flight darkened the sky, where now one of them is rarely seen.

Chapter Twenty-One
The Fight with Slavery

ALMOST from the beginning Ohio was called the Yankee state by her Southern neighbors. Burr had found her people too plodding for him, as he said, and it would not have been strange if the older slaveholding communities on her southern and eastern border had seen with distrust and dislike the advance of the young Free State and had given her that nickname partly out of envy and partly out of contempt. Their citizens were high-spirited and generous, but they had not the public spirit which New England had imparted to Ohio, for public spirit comes from equality and from the feeling for others' rights and the very supremacy which the slaveholders enjoyed was fatal to this feeling. Virginia and Kentucky were rich in independent character, but public spirit is better than this, for it cares for the independence of all through the self-sacrifice of each. That was the secret which Ohio early learned from New England and which kept her safe from slavery when it pressed so hard upon her in the friendship as well as the enmity of her neighbors.

We know that the Northwestern Territory was devoted to freedom by the law that created it, but we have seen that slavery was kept out of Ohio by one vote only when her first constitution was adopted and for a very long time there was a very large party favorable to slavery in our state.

It will seem strange to many of my readers that Ohio people of color were once not only not allowed to vote, but were not allowed to give testimony in the courts of law. They were treated in this like the Southern slaves and in fact, there was really a sort of slaveholding in Ohio in spite of the law. In the river counties many farmers hired slaves from their masters in Virginia and Kentucky and when the Southerners traveled through Ohio, they brought their slaves into the state with them and took them out again. But when the conscience of the Northern people began to stir against slavery, the Ohio abolitionists coaxed away the slaves of these Southern travelers and sojourners and this, with the constant escape of runaway slaves by their help, infuriated the friends of slavery inside as well as outside of the state. The abolitionists had what they called the Underground Railroad with stations at their houses in town and country and they sped the fugitives from one to another till they reached Canada. Their enemies accused them of tempting slaves across the Ohio in order to give them their freedom and in a little while the rage against them broke out in mobs and riots.

It would not be easy to trace here the course of events which led to these outbreaks. It is no doubt true that the abolitionists were often rash, if not reckless and that when they were maddened by the coldness or the hostility of the people to the cause of human freedom they did not stop at some acts which, though they were righteous enough, were unlawful. It was unlawful to harbor runaway slaves, but they did it gladly, and they appealed to the passions as well as the consciences of men in their hate of the sum of all villainies, as John Wesley called slavery. They not only met their foes half way, they carried the war into the hearts and homes of the enemy. From time to time wicked and sorrowful things happened to fret their fanaticism and keep it at a white heat. Peaceable negroes were attacked in their homes by ruffian whites, their cattle killed, their fields wasted; and sometimes they made a bloody resistance. They were not always harmless and they were not always pleasant neighbors. Slavery was a bad school, for the slaves as well as the masters and the Negroes, when not vicious and dishonest, were degraded and ignorant, for the public schools were shut against them and they could not read, any more than they could vote or bear witness. So it is not strange that they should have been hunted and harried everywhere in Southern Ohio.

In Pike County a whole neighborhood was invaded and several lives were lost before one of these foolish and wicked persecutions ended. This incident, which was one of many more or less violent, occurred in 1830 and two years later something still more tragical happened. A Negro calling himself Thomas Marshall, who had lived several years at Dayton, was caught up in the streets of that town by some men who, when his cries brought the citizens to his help, declared that he was a runaway slave. They took him before a magistrate and proved their charge; but one of the slave catchers held out the hope that his master would sell him. The poor slave gave fifty dollars himself toward his freedom and his ransom was well made up when word came from his owner in Kentucky that he would not part with him for any sum. His captors then took Marshall to Cincinnati where he was lodged for safe keeping over night in the fourth story of a hotel. When his guards fell asleep, the slave rose and threw himself out of the window to the ground fifty feet below. He was taken up fatally hurt and he died at dawn.

The anti-slavery meetings were often broken in upon by mobs and sometimes broken up. One of these riots took place in 1834 at Granville, in Licking County, where the Ohio Anti-slavery Convention held its anniversary in a barn on the outskirts. The members were returning to the village in a procession when the mob met them and at sight of the ladies among them shouted, "Egg the squaws!" and began to pelt them with eggs and other missiles while some ran and tried to trip them up. Many of the men were beaten and egged and the manes and tails of their horses were shaved. This was a favorite argument with the friends of slavery and if shaving horses' manes and tails could have availed, their party would easily have won.

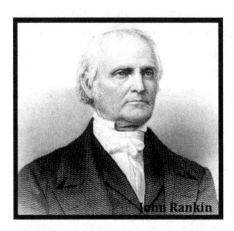

John Rankin

Some of the anti-slavery speakers and lecturers came on missions from the Eastern States, but several of the fiercest and bravest were like the Rev. John Rankin of Clermont County who had emigrated from Tennessee to Ohio because he would not live in a slaveholding community. He used to preach against slavery at frequent peril of his life and his son tells how a mob leader once mounted to his pulpit and threatened him with his club. "Stop speaking or I will burst your head," he shouted, but Rankin went quietly on as if nothing had been said and one of his friends dragged the ruffian from his side. Of course, he was always coming home with his horse's mane and tail shaved and of course his house was a station on the Underground Railroad to freedom.

James G. Birney

One of the boldest of the abolitionists was James G. Birney, who like Rankin had come to Ohio from the South. He started a newspaper called *The Philanthropist* in Cincinnati and for three months attacked slavery unsparingly in it. Then, on the 23d of July, 1836, the mob rose, broke into the printing office, threw the types into the street, tore down the press and cast the fragments into the river. Then they assailed the black people living in one of the alleys and shots were exchanged but no lives were lost. A few years later, however, in 1841, a general assault was made upon the Negroes by the mob; several on both sides were killed and many wounded and the office of *The Philanthropist* was again destroyed. Of course these things did not stop the fight against slavery, and it did not help slavery at all when the authorities of Lane Theological Seminary at Cincinnati forbade the students to write or to talk about it. That was foolish and useless; it only hurt the seminary and drove many students from it to the college at Oberlin, then newly founded in the woods of Lorain County. There, they could not only discuss slavery, but they could learn about it at first hand from the Negro students. The founders of Oberlin were not abolitionists but it is related that when they took Christ for their guide, they found that they could not shut out the friendless people whom the law kept from the schools, the polls, and the courts.

These few scattered facts will give some notion of the bitter feeling that prevailed during the first ten or twelve years of the fight against slavery in Ohio. Afterwards it became less intense as slavery became a political question between the two great parties of that day, the Whigs and the Democrats. Neither party expected to abolish slavery, but the

Whigs hoped to keep it out of the territories and all the new states. Both parties split upon this question at last and in 1856 the anti-slavery Whigs and anti-slavery Democrats joined in forming the Republican party, which in 1860 elected Abraham Lincoln upon its promise to shut slavery up to the states where it already existed.

But it must not be supposed, because the first bitter feeling had passed away, that the facts were changed or that the tragedies and outrages had ceased. After the passage of the Fugitive Slave Law in 1850, there was a new hunt for runaways all over the state and business on the Underground Railroad was never so brisk.

The hatred of slavery was revived in all its intensity by such cases as that of Margaret Gorden in 1856. This unhappy mother had escaped from Kentucky with her four children to the house of a free colored man below Mill Creek in Hamilton County, where they remained concealed with thirteen other fugitives. One night the place was suddenly attacked by the slave hunters under the lead of the United States officers. A fight followed and several on both sides were wounded, but at last the slaves were overpowered. While the officers were dragging the others from the house, Margaret seized a knife from the table and killed her little daughter rather than see her taken back to slavery, and then turned the bloody weapon against herself, but failed in the attempt on her own life. She was taken to Cincinnati and tried, not for murder, but for escaping from slavery together with the other fugitives, who said they would "go singing to the gallows," if only they need not go back to the South. They were all found guilty of seeking to be free and were returned to their owners. On her way down the river it is said that Margaret jumped from the boat with one of her remaining little ones in her arms. The child was drowned but Margaret was saved for the fate which she dreaded, and which she had twice risked her own and her children's life to shun. What became of her at last was never known. It is only known that she was carried back to her owner. She had two deep scars on her black face. At her trial she was asked what made them and she answered "White man struck me."

In Champaign County, a fugitive slave named Ad White resisted the attempt of the slave hunters to take him in 1857 and fired upon one of the United States marshals, whose life was saved by the Negro's bullet striking against the marshal's gun barrel. The people and their officers took the slave's side and the case was fought in and out of court. The sheriff of the county was brutally beaten with a slungshot by the marshal who had so narrowly escaped death himself and never fully recovered. But at last the slave's master offered to take a thousand dollars for him. The money was promptly raised and paid over, and White lived on unmolested.

As late as the summer of 1860 a fugitive slave was arrested near Iberia, in Morrow County. A party of young men caught one of the marshals and shaved his head, while others beat his comrades. Rev. Mr. Gordon, President of Ohio Central College, stood by trying to prevent the punishment but he alone was arrested. He was sentenced to prison, where he lay till Lincoln pardoned him. The pardon did not recognize his innocence and he would not leave his cell until his friends forced him to do so. By this time the damp jail air had infected him and he died, shortly after, of consumption.

One would think that such things as these would have cured the Ohio people of all sentiment for slavery for they had no real interest in it. But even in the second year of the Civil War, which the love of slavery had stirred up against the Union, the famous antislavery orator, Wendell Phillips, was stoned and egged while trying to lecture in Cincinnati. Before this time, however, events had gone so far that there was no staying them.

John Brown

One of the earliest and most chief of these events was the attempt of John Brown to free the slaves in Virginia. He had already fought slavery in Kansas where it was trying to invade free soil, and in 1859 he thought that the time had come to carry the war into the enemy's country. He did this by placing himself with a small force of daring young men, several of his own sons among the rest, in the mountains near Harper's Ferry. He hoped that when he had seized the United States Arsenal at that point and given them arms the slaves would join him and help to fight their way to the free states under his lead. But when they were attacked in the Arsenal, Brown and his men were easily overpowered by a detachment of Marines* sent from Washington. Several of his followers were killed; a few escaped; the rest suffered death with their leader on the gallows at Charlestown.

*These Marines were under the command of Col. Robert E. Lee, future Confederate General.

Some think that Brown was mad, some that he was inspired, some that he was right, some that he was wrong. But whatever men think of him, there are none who doubt that he was a hero, ready to shed his blood for the cause he held just. His name can never die, so long as the name of America lives and it is part of the fame of Ohio that he dwelt many years in our state. For many years of his younger manhood Brown had lived at Hudson, in Summit County. For months before his attempt in

Virginia, he and his men were coming and going at different points in the Western Reserve and in Ashtabula County, where one of his sons then had a farm, he kept hidden the pikes with which he hoped to arm slaves. One of the young men who died with him on the scaffold at Charlestown was the Quaker lad, Edwin Coppock, of Columbiana County who wrote, two days before he suffered, a touching letter of farewell to his friends. "I had fondly hoped to live to see the principles of the Declaration of Independence fully realized; I had hoped to see the dark stain of slavery blotted from our land. But two more short days remain to me to fulfill my earthly destiny. At the expiration of those days I shall stand upon the scaffold to take my last look of earthly scenes. But that scaffold has but little dread for me, for I honestly believe that I am innocent of any crime justifying such a punishment. But by the taking of my life and the lives of my comrades, Virginia is but hastening on the day when the slave will rejoice in his freedom."

Chapter Twenty-Two

The Civil War in Ohio

THOUGH the Ohio people were too plodding for Aaron Burr and though they were taunted almost from the first as the Yankee state of the West, they seem to have had war in their blood, which may have been their heritage from the long struggle with the Indians. But after the peace with Great Britain in 1815 there was no war cloud in the Ohio sky until Morgan swept across our horizon with his hard-riders, except at one time in 1835.

There had then arisen between our state authorities and those of Michigan a dispute concerning the border line between the two commonwealths and matters went so far that the governors of both States called out their militia. The Michigan troops actually invaded Ohio and overran the watermelon patches near Toledo, ate the chickens of the neighborhood, destroyed an ice house and carried off one Ohioan prisoner. But the mere terror of the Ohio name sufficed to send them flying home again when they heard that our riflemen were waiting for them in Toledo and many deserters from their ranks took to the woods on their way back. This vindicated the glory of our state. We cheerfully submitted when the arbitrators chosen to settle the dispute decided it mainly in favor of Michigan and we have ever since lived at peace with that commonwealth.

All this seems now like a huge joke and so it has ever since been regarded, but a war was coming which was serious enough. It might be said that the great Civil War began with "John Brown's invasion of Virginia," in 1859, but it might just as well be said that it began with the fighting for and against freedom in Kansas in 1856. In fact it might be said that it began with the mobbing of anti-slavery speakers and the rescue of runaway slaves all over the North from 1830 onwards. Yet this would be fantastic, even if it were true, and we had better accept the dates which history gives. In 1860 Abraham Lincoln was elected President by the men opposed to the spread of slavery and in 1861 the slave states, feeling that their mastery of the Union was gone, left it one after another and the first fighting took place through the effort of the United States government to hold its forts in the South.

In this war, Ohio played so great a part that it is hard for Ohio people to keep from claiming that she played the first part. Remembering that General Grant, General Sherman, General Sheridan, the three greatest soldiers of the war, were all Ohio men, we might be tempted to claim that without these the war would not have been won for the Union. But it is safer to claim nothing more than that Ohio gave the nation the generals who won the war. Our three greatest soldiers were only chief among many others under whose lead Ohio sent to the war some three hundred and twenty thousand men, during the four years of fighting, a force almost as great as that of whole nations in other times.

Ohio men shed their blood on all the battlefields of the South, but only once was the war which consumed her children by tens of thousands brought home to her own hearths. This was when the state was invaded by John Morgan and his hard-riders in 1863. Morgan was born at Huntsville in Alabama and was of the true Southern type...gallant, reckless, independent. He was one of the bravest and luckiest chiefs of Confederate cavalry, and when he was ordered to march northward from Tennessee through Kentucky and attempt the capture of Louisville, but not to pass the Ohio, he trusted to his fortune and crossed the river into Indiana at the head of some twenty-three hundred horsemen.

On the 13th of July he entered the state of Ohio, a few miles north of Cincinnati and passed eastward unmolested by the Union General Burnside, who preferred not to bring him to battle in the neighborhood of the city, but to wait some chance of attacking him elsewhere. The militia had been called out by the governor and the whole country was on the alert. But Morgan's men passed through Clermont, Brown, Adams, Pike, Jackson, Vinton, Athens, and Gallia counties into Meigs with comparatively little molestation, though the militia learned rapidly to embarrass if not to imperil his course.

His men suffered terribly in their long ride. They had to live on the country as best they could and they were literally dropping with sleep as they pushed their jaded horses along the roads, everywhere threatened by the Ohio sharpshooters. They fell from their saddles and were left behind; they crawled off in the darkness and threw themselves down in the woods and fields, glad to awaken as prisoners in the hands of their pursuers. At first the large towns were alarmed by the fear of pillage but Morgan had hardly got into Ohio before it became his chief aim to get out again. His hard-riders were confined in their depredations mainly to the plunder of the country stores on their route. They stole what they could, but they stole without method or reason, except in the matter of horses, which they really needed and could use. They commonly left their worn-out chargers in exchange, but they took the freshest and strongest horses they could get, at any rate. In their horse stealing they were not so very unlike the Kentucky pioneers who used to cross into the Ohio country for the ponies of the Indians, and they practiced it at much the same risk; for the Ohio people were becoming every moment madder and more mischievous. At first they only cut down trees to check Morgan's march after he got by but they soon began to obstruct the roads in front of him; and though they burned one bridge over a river that he could easily ford, it was not long before they learned to destroy bridges where the streams were otherwise impassable.

By the time he reached Portland the militia were closing in around him and the next morning two detachments of United States cavalry struck him, while the gunboats which had been watching for him on the river, opened fire on him. In a few minutes the fight was over. Morgan left seven hundred of his men prisoners behind him and with twelve hundred others fled north and east to seek a new way out of Ohio. The fight at Buffington Island took place on the 18th, five days after Morgan crossed the Ohio line into Hamilton County and on the 26th he surrendered with the constantly lessening remnant of his force seven miles from New Lisbon in Columbiana County.

The prisoners were all sent for safe keeping to the penitentiary at Columbus but on the night of November 7th, Morgan and six of his comrades made their escape by digging into an air-space under the floor of his cell with their table-knives, passing through this to the prison walls, and letting themselves down with ropes made of their bed-clothes.

At the station where they were to take the train for Cincinnati, Morgan was dismayed to realize that he had no money to buy a ticket but one of his officers had been supplied by a young lady who sent him some bank notes concealed in a book. They rode all night in great fear and anxiety and just before the train drew into Cincinnati they put on the brakes and slowed it enough to drop from it with safety. Then they lost no time in making for the Ohio River where they hired a boy to set them over to Kentucky in his boat. Morgan had not found the Ohio people too plodding for him, as Aaron Burr had, but he was quite as glad to leave their state, which he never revisited, for he was killed the next year in Tennessee.

He left behind him in Ohio by no means a wholly evil name, and some stories are told of him that more than hint at a generous nature. A Union soldier, whom his men had taken, tried to break his musket across a stone and one of the Confederate officers drew his pistol to shoot him. Morgan forbade it. "Never harm a man who has surrendered," he said. "He was only doing what I should have done in his place."

We may be sure that such an enemy inflicted no wanton injury upon the country and there was something in Morgan's presence that corresponded with this magnanimity of his character. He was a man of powerful frame, large beyond the common, of great endurance, and able to outride any of his men, without sleep or rest. He had a fresh complexion with fair hair and beard and his face was rather mild. When he gave himself up at last, it was with an apparently cheerful unconcern at the turn of luck which in other raids had enabled him to break bridges, capture trains, and destroy millions of value in military stores.

Ohio is herself built upon so grand a scale that even her enemies seem to have been cast in a noble mold and the jokes upon her own people that form the life of most of the stories of Morgan's raid are as large as he. At one point, forty miles from their line of march, a good lady saved the family horse from the southern troopers by locking him into the parlor where his stamping on the hollow floor kept the neighborhood awake the whole night through.

One of Morgan's men, who plundered wildly but not very wickedly, carried for two days a bird cage with three canaries in it. Another, at the looting of a country store, filled his pockets with bone-buttons. They were only dangerous when they met reluctance in their frequent horse trades. They called at the house of a gentleman in Hamilton County at one o'clock in the morning, and asked for breakfast. When he objected that there was no fire at that time, they suggested that they could kindle one for him that it might be hard to put out. Then he made one himself and they got their breakfast.

In Carroll County, Morgan himself called for dinner at the house of a lady whose maiden name was Morgan and at table they fell into such kindly chat about their cousinship that she ended by giving him a clean shirt, which he needed badly, and gratefully wore away.

A farmer in Morgan County took refuge in his pigpen where one of the raiders found him trying to hide behind a fat mother of a family who was suckling her farrow. The raider grinned: "Hello! How did you get here? Did you all come in the same litter?"

A stuttering hero who had been bragging of what he would do to the enemy if he got at them, was surprised by Morgan's men with a demand for his surrender. He flung up his hands instantly. "I s-s-surrendered f-f-f-five minutes ago!"

One of the greatest jokes of all was played upon a friend of the South in Hamilton County. My younger readers may not suppose that there could be any friends of the South in Ohio at that time, but in truth there were a great many...and far more than there were at the outbreak of the war. Then most of us believed that it would be quickly fought to an end, but after it had dragged on for two years, when its drain on the blood and the money of the nation was severest and the end seemed as far off as at the beginning, those who had never loved the cause of freedom could easily blow the smoldering fires of discontent into a wide and far-raging flame. It must not be imagined that the Northern enemies of the North were all bad men. They were sometimes men of conscience and sincerely opposed to the war against the South as unjust and hopeless. But they were called copperheads, because for a long time they lurked silently among the people, like that deadly snake which used to haunt the grass of the backwoods and bite without warning. They were still called copperheads when they lifted their heads and struck boldly at the Union cause under the lead of a very able man, Clement L. Vallandigham, (Whom we shall presently learn more of) and it was an old copperhead who followed Morgan's rear guard with the best horse the hard-riders had left him and who tried to get speech with the officer in command. He explained that he was a follower of Vallandigham and against the war, and he pleaded that on this ground he ought to have his horses back. The Morgan Colonel said they could not stop to listen but they would hear him if he would drive along with them. He added that as some of his soldiers were worn out, the copperhead had better give them his wagon and when the copperhead said that he could not ride, the Colonel answered that he should be allowed to walk. After walking awhile, he complained that his boots hurt him and the Colonel ordered them taken off. The copperhead was obliged to follow in his stockings till the raiders camped. Then, to amuse their leisure, they taught him a Morgan song, and obliged him to dance, fat and fagged as he was, to his own music, while they applauded him with shouts of "Go it, old Yank! Louder!" till their commanding officer ordered them to harness a worn-out crow bait to his wagon and bring him three wretched jades for the horses he wanted to recover, and let him go.

It is not known whether this behavior of his friends turned the copperheads against them or not. But in spite of the Morgan raid, and in spite of all the reasons and victories of a North, the largest vote that the Democratic party had ever polled, up to that time, was cast in favor of a man who had been bitterest against the war and who was then in exile from his native country because of his treasonable words and practices. Even three thousand soldiers in the field voted for him and this is far more surprising than that forty thousand voted against him. As we look back through the perspective of history, our state seems to have been solid for the Union and for freedom; but this is an appearance only and it is better that we should realize the truth. It will do no harm even to realize that the man who embodied the copperhead feeling was by no means a malignant man, however mistaken.

Clement Vallandigham

Clement Laird Vallandigham was born in 1820 at New Lisbon, of mixed Huguenot and Scotch-Irish ancestry, a stock which has given us some of our best and greatest men. His father was a Presbyterian minister who eked out his poor salary by teaching a classical school in his own house. Clement was ready for college long before he was old enough to be received and when he was graduated from Jefferson College, at Cannonsburg in Pennsylvania, he came back to New Lisbon and began to practice law.

So far all the influences of his life should have been at least as good for the generous side of politics as for the ungenerous, but from the first he cast his lot with the oppressor. In 1845 he was sent to the legislature where he took a leading part in opposing the repeal of the Black Laws, which kept the Negro from voting at the polls or testifying in the courts. Two years later he fixed his home in Dayton where he quickly came to the front as a State's Rights Democrat in the full Southern sense. He was given, by a Democratic house, the seat to which Lewis D. Campbell was elected in 1856 and he remained in Congress till defeated in 1862. Up to the last moment he never ceased to vote and to speak against the war, because he believed it impossible to conquer the South and when he came back to Ohio he kept on saying what he believed.

This brought him under condemnation of General Order No. 38, issued by General Burnside at Cincinnati, forbidding any person to express sympathy for the enemy under pain of being sent out of the Union lines into the lines of the Confederates. Vallandigham defied this order. He was arrested by a company of the 115th Ohio and taken to Cincinnati from Dayton where a mob of his friends broke out the next day and burned the office of the leading Republican newspaper. General Burnside sent a force and quelled the mob and promptly had Vallandigham tried by a court-martial which sentenced him to imprisonment in Fort Warren at Boston during the war. President Lincoln changed this sentence to transportation through our lines into the borders of the Southern Confederacy and Vallandigham was hurried by special train from Cincinnati to Murfreesboro in Tennessee, where General Rosecrans was in command.

In a long interview, General Rosecrans tried to convince him of his wrongdoing and asked if he did not know that but for his protection the soldiers would tear him to pieces in an instant. Vallandigham answered, "Draw your soldiers up in a hollow square tomorrow morning and announce to them that Vallandigham desires to vindicate himself. And I will guarantee that when they have heard me through, they will be more willing to tear Lincoln and yourself to pieces than they will Vallandigham."

The general said he had too much regard for his prisoner's life to try it but the charm of the man had won upon him. "He don't look a bit like a traitor, now, does he, Joe?" he remarked to one of his staff, and he warmly shook hands with Vallandigham when they parted at two o'clock on the morning of May 25.

Vallandigham mounted into the spring wagon provided for the rest of his journey and was driven rapidly out of the sleeping town toward the Confederate lines. It was still in the forenoon when, in response to a Federal flag of truce, Colonel Webb of the 51st Alabama sent word to say that he was ready to receive him. Two Federal officers crossed the enemy's lines with him where he was met by one private soldier, and after some hours taken into the presence of the commander. General Bragg received him very kindly at Shelbyville and allowed him to report on parole at Wilmington, North Carolina. There, he took a blockade runner for Nassau, where he found a steamer for Canada.

He arrived in the British province early in July to find that the Ohio Democrats had nominated him for governor and that his party throughout the country had expressed its sympathy with him. President Lincoln met one of their committees and agreed with them that Vallandigham's arrest was unusual, but he quaintly added, "He could not be persuaded that the government should not take measures in time of war which must not be taken in time of peace, any more than he could be persuaded that a sick man must not take medicine which was not good food for a well one."

So thought the great majority of the Ohio people, who duly chose John Brough, a War Democrat, for their governor in October. Vallandigham remained in Canada until 1864 when he returned to Dayton where he was warmly received by his friends and not molested by the authorities. But he had never afterwards any political importance in spite of his great abilities and the peculiar charm of his manner for all kinds of people. After the war was over, he accepted its conclusions with earnest good faith and three years later he met his death by a curious accident. He was showing a friend, in behalf of a client in whom he was greatly interested, how a pistol might go off in a pocket and cause a mortal wound such as his client was accused of inflicting on another. The pistol in his hand was really discharged. Vallandigham was fatally wounded and died shortly afterwards.

Chapter Twenty-Three
Famous Ohio Soldiers

FIRST among these I count the great chief Pontiac who led the rebellion of the mid-western tribes against the English after the French had abandoned them and who was born in Auglaize County. I count the renowned chief Tecumseh too, that later and lesser Pontiac, who attempted to do against the Americans what Pontiac tried to do against the English.

It was some time before the great white men of Ohio began to be born here but in the meanwhile there were those born elsewhere who, like General Harrison, became Ohioans and so did what they could to repair the defect of birth. There is no reason to think that such men were shaped by Ohio influences but it is the habit of our generous Ohio state patriotism to claim as Ohioans not only those who were born here, and those who came to live here, but those who were born here and then went to live elsewhere.

Valiant and able generals came from the different parts of Ohio and from the different races which settled there. But the Scotch race, descending through New England, has the highest place in our soldiers' ancestry and the county of Clermont has the deathless glory of being the birthplace of Ulysses Simpson Grant, one of the greatest captains of all time, one of the purest patriots, one of the best and gentlest men. I need not speak of his career as a soldier for that has become a part of the nation's history. The beginnings of his life were rude and hard. It was afterwards often clouded with failure. It brightened out into such splendid success as few lives have ever known; it was again darkened by trouble and disaster, and it closed in a long anguish of suffering. But if ever a life was worth living it was his and his memory is safe forever in the love of his country and the honor of the world.

His parents removed soon after he was born to Brown County, where Georgetown was his home until he was sent to West Point at seventeen. His whole boyhood, therefore, was spent in Southwestern Ohio where a boy may live the happiest life on earth and where Grant played, worked, planned and studied not only without a dream of the place he was to take in history, but without special thought or liking for the calling in which he was to stand with Caesar and with Napoleon.

Ulysses S. Grant

When he was eight years old, be began to work in his father's tannery where he drove the horse that turned the bark mill and broke the bark into the hopper. He did not like the work and he escaped from it when he could and did jobs of wagoning about the village. He loved his horses and kept them sleek and fat; and it is told of him that when he first traded horses he was so eager to get a certain colt that he offered the man even more than he asked.

He was fond of all boyish sports, but he was never rough or profane or foul-mouthed and he was noted among his mates for his truth and honesty. The girls liked him for his gentleness, the younger children for his kindness. He never teased them and he never tormented any living creature. There may have been better boys, but I have never heard of them, and if Grant passed only his first seventeen years in his native state, they were years of as true greatness relatively as any that followed. From the first, he was self-reliant and taught himself to trust to his own powers and resources. When seven years old, he got an unbroken colt from the stable in his father's absence, hitched it to a sled which he loaded with wood in the forest and then drove home with a single line. He once wished to ride his father's pacer on an errand he was sent upon, but his father could not spare it and the boy took his colt. "I will break him to pace," he said. And he came back with the colt pacing. At twelve he hauled logs with a heavy draft team. Once the men who were to load for him did not come and Grant managed with the help of a fallen tree to get the logs on the truck alone and drove home with them. After eleven he had scarcely any schooling except that of hard work, until he was appointed to West Point.

From Georgetown, another Ohioan famous in the Great War was sent about the same time to the Naval Academy at Annapolis. This was the boy Daniel Ammen, who was destined to become Admiral Ammen. He had saved Grant's life when they were bathing together in White Oak Creek and Grant remembered him with his high office and title when he became President.

But Ammen had won both by his services during the war for the Ammens were fighters. The Admiral's brother Jacob had early distinguished himself by gallantry that won him a generalship. Long before this their father had begun the good fight by printing John Rankin's letters against slavery in his newspaper at Ripley.

Daniel McCook

From Carroll County came that wonderful race of fighters, the McCooks. Daniel McCook, Presbyterian elder and Sunday-school superintendent, went into the war at sixty-three with his sons, and two years later was killed in the engagement with Morgan at Buffington

Island. Latimer A. McCook died in 1869 of wounds received during his service as surgeon in the battles of the war. General Robert Latimer McCook was murdered by guerrillas as he lay sick and wounded near Salem, Alabama, in 1862. General A. McDowell McCook was a West Pointer who won his major generalship by his gallantry at Shiloh. General Daniel McCook, Jr., led the assault at Kenesaw Mountain, where he was mortally wounded. Edwin Stanton McCook was graduated at Annapolis, but preferred the land service, and rose to the rank of brevet major general, through the courage and ability he had shown at Fort Henry, at Fort Donelson, at Chickamauga, and in Sherman's March to the Sea. Charles Morris McCook was killed at the first Bull Run in 1861, while in his freshman year at Gambier. His father saw him overwhelmed by the enemy and called out to him to surrender; but he answered "Father, I will never surrender to a rebel," and was shot down by one of the Black Horse Cavalry. John J. McCook served in the campaigns of the West and with Grant from the battle of the Wilderness onward to the end. He was severely wounded at Shady Grove, and left the army with the rank of colonel.

Dr. John McCook, another Sunday-school superintendent, was the father of Edwin Moody McCook, who rendered brilliant service early in the war and left the army at its close with the rank of major general. His greatest exploit was breaking through the enemy's lines before Sherman began his march to the sea, and effecting a diversion by the damage he did and the prisoners he took. His brother Anson George McCook was at the first Bull Run and in the great battles of the Southwest, and was brevetted Brigadier General at the end of the war. Rev. Henry C. McCook enlisted first as a private soldier and became chaplain of a regiment, but did no actual fighting. He is well known as a naturalist and theologian, and his youngest brother John James is distinguished as a linguist. His brother left the army as colonel after seeing some of the first fighting and became an Episcopal minister. Roderick Sheldon McCook left Annapolis in 1859 and promptly shared in the capture of a slaver off the African coast. From 1861 to 1865 he was engaged in all the naval movements at Newbern, Wilmington, Charleston, Fort Fisher, and on the James, and suffered lasting injury to his health on the monitors. He left the navy with the rank of commodore. All these McCooks, except the Rev. J. J.

McCook, now professor in Trinity College, Hartford, remained of the Presbyterian faith, which seems natural to their Scotch-Irish race.

Hayes

Of all the Americans who have lived, none is securer of lasting remembrance than Rutherford B. Hayes, who was born in Delaware, October 4, 1822. He was a great lawyer, a great soldier, a great statesman, a great philanthropist, a man without taint or stain. He had to suffer the doubt thrown by his enemies upon his right to the high office they had themselves conceded to him, but he was never wounded in his own conscience or in the love of the people. He was three times governor of Ohio, and when he became President of the United States he devoted himself to healing the hurts left by the war he had helped to fight. He made the North and South friends in the love he had for both sections, and then he gladly laid down his charge and went back to private life, after giving the country peace with honor. His presidency was not only one of the most distinguished and enlightened statesmanship, but it was consecrated by the virtues of the woman who made the White House the happiest home in the land. Lucy Webb Hayes, who had been like a mother to the soldiers of her husband's command, gave the social side of his administration the grace and charm of her surpassingly wise and lovely character. He never knew in his youth the poverty and hard work which narrowed the early life of Grant and Garfield. He was born to comfort and lived in greater and greater affluence; he had only to profit by his opportunities, while they had to make theirs; but he did profit by them. From school to college, and from college to the study of law, he passed easily successful in all that he tried to do, and he always tried to do his duty. Like Grant, he was of farther Scotch and nearer New England origin, but the next most distinguished native of Delaware County was of Dutch stock, as his name witnesses.

William Starke Rosecrans was born in 1819, and entered West Point when only fifteen years old. He was in civil life when the war broke out in 1861, but of course he at once took part in it, and fought through a series of most brilliant campaigns, without one defeat, until the battle of Chickamauga in 1863. Even this he won, but the trust President Lincoln had felt in him and expressed up to the last moment was shaken by Rosecrans's enemies, and lie was removed from his command. He left the army with the rank of major general, and he held afterwards places of high honor, but he felt that the wrong done him was never atoned for. Twenty-five years after his removal he told a meeting of his old comrades the touching story of how the stroke fell and how he bore it. "It was at night that I received the order, and I sent for General Thomas," who was to replace him. "He came to the tent and took his seat. I handed him the letter. He read it and as he did so his breast began to swell and he turned pale. He did not want to accept the command, but we agreed on consideration that he must do so, and I told him that I could not bear to meet my troops afterwards. 'I want to leave,' I said, 'before the announcement is made, and I will start early in the morning.' I packed up that night, and early in the morning, about seven o'clock, I rode away through the fog that then hung over the camp."

William Tecumseh Sherman, who was born at Lancaster, Fairfield County, in 1820, was like his comrade and beloved friend Grant in the poverty he was born to. But his family was of historical distinction, while Grant's had always been obscure, and his father died a judge of the Supreme Court of Ohio. As he died poor, his large family of children were left to their mother, whose means were not equal to their maintenance and education. Thomas Ewing, the great man of the place, had been the father's friend, and he wished to adopt "the smartest of the children." It is not known how his choice fell upon Sherman, who was playing with some other boys on a sand bank near Ewing's house when it was made, and had apparently nothing to do with it.

William Tecumseh Sherman

His father had called him Tecumseh because he admired the Indian chief's noble character and his merciful treatment of prisoners, and because he wished the boy to be a soldier. Ewing fulfilled the father's wish by appointing the son to a West Point cadetship at sixteen. Sherman had meantime fallen in love with Miss Ellen Ewing, and he married her in 1850. Then he left the army and tried banking and the law, but liked neither, and he was President of the Louisiana state military academy when the Civil War began. With his frank, bold, impetuous nature, he forewarned the governor that he should side with the Union, and he asked to be notified in time before the state seceded.

He received the surrender of the last great Confederate army, after a series of the most splendid strokes of generalship. His March to the Sea will be forever famous. The highest British military criticism pronounced his attempt "the most brilliant or the most foolish thing ever attempted by a military leader," and we all know how it turned out. Grant called him "the best field officer the war had produced," and there has been nothing in history more sweet and beautiful than the friendship between these two great men. They were unlike in everything but their unselfishness and single-hearted patriotism, and they trusted as wholly as they loved each other.

Irvin McDowell, born at Franklinton, Franklin County, in 1818, was the brave and gifted officer who lost the first battle of Bull Run, where he failed less ruinously than any other general of that moment of the war would have done. His name and fame have outlived that disaster, though the people did not then know enough to forgive him for his army's defeat. He was again of that tough Scotch-Irish breed that so many

Ohioans are of; like our other great generals, he was a West Pointer, and he was of the high and kindly personal character common to them.

Custer

George A. Custer put into his life of vivid action the splendor of romance. His figure stands foremost in any picture of the war as that of the most dashing and daring cavalier of his time; but if his bearing was that of a young hero of fiction, his deeds were those of an accomplished and disciplined modern soldier. He was born at New Rumley in Harrison County, of a Hessian ancestor who had come over to fight for King George against the country which Custer lived and died to serve, and he inherited from him the blue German eyes, and the yellow German hair which he loved to wear long, and flying about his neck in his gallant charges. But otherwise he was of the simple matter-of-fact Ohio character. He got himself sent to West Point by means of a letter which he wrote to the congressman of his district. He frankly owned himself "a Democrat boy," and though the congressman was a Republican his fancy was taken with the honesty of the youth, whom he never saw till one day a young officer "with long yellow hair, hanging like Absalom's," presented himself at his house in Washington as Lieutenant Custer. "Mr. Bingham, I've been in my first battle," he said, "and I've come to tell you I've tried not to show the coward." After that, in numberless bold forays and fierce battles, he displayed such dauntless bravery, such brilliant prowess, that General Sheridan, in sending Mrs. Custer the table on which Lee signed his surrender, could write, "I know of no person more instrumental in bringing about this desirable event than your own most gallant husband." All the world knows how this glorious hero fell in the West, long after the war, before an overwhelming force of Indians.

Garfield

If Custer was the romance of our history, James A. Garfield was its tragedy, the sort of noble tragedy which exalts while it awes. Again we have in his life the story, so often told in the Ohio annals, of early struggles with poverty, and of triumph over unfriendly fate. The child who was born in the rude farmhouse in Orange, Cuyahoga County, in 1831, was of Puritan lineage on his father's side and Huguenot blood on his mother's; and throughout his life he showed the qualities of both strains. He was left the youngest of four children to the care of his widowed mother, soon after his birth, and at the very beginning his blithe and dauntless spirit felt the stress of want. But he began to help himself and school himself, as the children of the poor must and do, and he early showed a passion for literature and adventure; he wanted to read; he wanted to go to sea; he actually tried to ship on a schooner at Cleveland, but, failing this, he got a chance to drive a canal-boat team. He fell sick and came home, and when he got well he learned carpentering. With his earnings in that trade he helped himself through the Academy at Chardon in Geauga County. From there he went to Hiram College, in Portage County, and then to Williams College, in Massachusetts. He studied law, and was elected to the Ohio Senate, which he left to enter the army. He was a brave and able soldier, and rose from lieutenant to be major general, before he left the service of his country in the field, to serve her in Congress. After sixteen years in the House, his state sent him to the Senate, and then his fellow-citizens chose him their President. He had been only four months in the White House, when the wretched Guiteau, a fool maddened by his own vanity and the sight of others' malevolence toward the man who never hated any one, shot him down;

and he lingered amidst the fervent sympathy of the whole world, till he died nine or ten weeks later. Of all the great Ohioans he was the gentlest and kindest nature; he never did harm to any man, and his heart was as high as his aspiring intellect above anything base or low. His ambition was in all things for what was fine and noble.

Quincy Adams Gilmore, who was born on a farm in Lorain County in 1825, was graduated at the head of his class from West Point. He achieved lasting fame in the siege of Fort Pulaski in Georgia, which other engineers had said could never be taken. Gilmore reduced it in two days by a feat in gunnery which changed forever the science and practice of that branch of the military art. In the ooze of a trembling marsh, which scarcely lifted its uncertain surface above the tides, he planted his heavy rifled cannon at three times the distance that siege artillery was believed effective, and battered down the walls of the fort with perfect ease, and with the loss of only one life in his command.

Philip H. Sheridan

The doubt as to the birthplace of Philip H. Sheridan, with a choice between Massachusetts, New York, and Ohio, seems not to have been felt by Sheridan himself. He decided that he was born in Somerset, Perry County, Ohio, in March, 1831, and there is no good reason to suppose that he did not know. While so many of our soldiers were of Scotch-Irish origin, he was simply of Irish origin, and his father and mother were poor Irish laboring people, Catholics in religion, and careful to rear their son in their faith. Many stories are told of his boyhood, which seems to have been like that of most other Ohio boys of his generation. The most significant of these stories are those relating to his childish love and knowledge of horses and horsemanship; for they seem the prophecy of the greatest cavalry commander of modern times, who invented that branch of the service anew, as Gilmore reinvented gunnery. Sheridan's first famous ride was on a barebacked, bridleless horse which he mounted in the pasture where it was feeding, and clung to with his knees and elbows in its long flight down the highway. No poet has yet put this legendary feat into verse, but all my readers know the poem which celebrates Sheridan's ride from Winchester to Cedar Creek. This ride not only saved the day, but it stamped with the fiery little man's character the history of the whole campaign in the Valley of the Shenandoah; and in it, as it were, he met Sherman halfway on his March to the Sea, and completed the deadly circuit in which the great rebellion died.

Of all our commanders he was perhaps the best beloved by his men, for he fought with his men. He tried to account for their liking him on no other ground. He once said, "These men all know that where it is the hottest there I am, and they like it, and that is the reason they like me." He was in the hottest place because he thought it was his duty to be there, and not because he was fearless. "The man who says he isn't afraid under fire, is a liar. I am afraid," he frankly said, with a touch of that profanity which Grant never used, "and if I followed my own impulse I should turn and get out. It is all a question of the power of mind over body."

As a boy he had some schooling at a Catholic school, under an eccentric Irish master whom he used to play tricks upon, and who used to thrash him impartially with the rest. When he left school, he became a clerk in a hardware store in his native village, and then in a dry-goods store. From the last place, he was appointed in 1848 to West Point and his destiny was fixed. In his class was another Ohio boy, born not far from Sheridan's birthplace, at the little town of Clyde, Sandusky County, in the year 1828. This was James B. McPherson, Scotch-Irish by race as his name shows, and, as his history was to show later, one of the worthiest scions of that soldier bearing stock. If Sheridan was the well-beloved of his men, McPherson was singularly dear to those who were closest to him and should have known him best. He was of a most affectionate nature, tenderly attached to his home and kindred, as men are apt to be if their homes are poor and their kindred have shared privation with them; but McPherson kept through all his prosperity and success the qualities which endear men to their fellows and comrades.

The noble friendship between Grant and Sherman is one of the most precious of our national memories, but these great commanders seem to have loved McPherson next after one another.

His father was a farmer who worked at the trade of blacksmithing when he was not following the plow; and the boy helped him in the field and at the forge. When James was thirteen, his father died, and then he got a place in a village store, and did what he could to support his widowed mother and orphan brothers and sisters. It is told that when he left them on the farm he ran tear-blinded till he got out of sight, and then sat down with his little bundle in the woods and cried with homesickness. But he went to work, and he studied and read in his hours of leisure, and when he got the promise of a nomination to West Point he managed to spend two terms at the Norwalk Academy in preparing himself. He was then so old that he was afraid he would not be admitted to West Point; but once in the army he seemed to regain his youth. When he took command of the Army of the Tennessee, under Sherman, he was only thirty-two years old.

In one of the battles before Atlanta, in July, 1864, he was fired upon by a Confederate skirmish line, while personally leading a movement of his troops, and received a mortal wound. He rode a little way into the woods to avoid capture, and then fell from his horse; and as he lay there dying alone a private of an Iowa regiment found him, and cared for him till he expired. Sherman's grief for his loss was open and passionate. He wept over his dead face, and in the report of his loss to headquarters he said, "Those whom he commanded loved him even to idolatry; and I, his associate and commander, fail in words adequate to express my opinion of his great worth." Grant wrote to McPherson's aged grandmother: "The nation had more to expect from him than from almost anyone living." He wished to express the grief of personal love for the departed, and he testified to "his zeal, his great, almost unequaled ability, his amiability, and all the manly virtues that can adorn a commander."

Such were the greatest of the great Ohio soldiers. To say that they were, each in his different way, the first soldiers of the war, is to keep well within the modest truth. They believed in one another, they trusted one another, for they knew one another. The love between them, impassioned in Sherman, frank and hearty in Sheridan, tender in McPherson, deep and constant in Grant, is one of the most beautiful facts of our history, or of any history, a feeling without one ungenerous quality. It was indeed —"A goodly fellowship of noble knights," such as has not been since that of King Arthur's Table Round.

Chapter Twenty-Four
Ohio Statesmen

THE men who have given distinction to our state in politics could hardly be more than named in a record like this; and I shall not try to speak of them all or try to keep any order in my mention of them except the alphabetical order of the counties where they were born, or where they lived.

From Ashtabula County, the names that will come at once to the reader's mind are those of Joshua R. Giddings and Benjamin F. Wade, both of a national fame inseparable from the history of the struggle with slavery. Giddings was first to cast his lot with the almost hopeless cause of freedom, but the fiery nature of Wade served to keep it warm in the hearts of its later adherents and to spread its light. Neither of these great Ohioans were Ohioans by birth. Giddings was born in Athens, Pennsylvania, in 1795, and came to Ashtabula County in 1806, where he dwelt until within a few years of his death, which took place at Montreal in 1864, while he was Consul General for Canada. He studied law, and succeeded at the bar before he entered political life. He was then twenty years in Congress as representative from the Ashtabula district, which promptly returned him when he was expelled from the House of Representatives for presenting a petition against slavery. His courage was so unconscious that he seemed never to assert it in his long career of defiance at Washington, but it never failed him in the presence of the dangers that often beset him there. In early life his people were desperately poor; he had scarcely a thought of school till he was twenty-three, and it was not until he had conquered from the wilderness a farm for his father and himself that he found time for study. He always loved the simplicity of the new country, and when he came home to the village of Jefferson from the sessions of Congress, he liked to "turn himself out to grass," as he called it: to put on old clothes and a straw hat, and walk barefoot through the streets which he had known when they were forest trails.

Wade was born at Hills Parish, Massachusetts, in 1800, and he too was born in utter poverty. He worked on a farm, and then worked with pick and spade on the Erie Canal; but by the time he was twenty-one he knew much science and philosophy through studies he had pursued in a woodchopper's hut by the light of pine knots. In Jefferson he read law and became Giddings's partner. He was sent to the United States Senate in 1851 as an antislavery Whig, and he continued to stand four-square for freedom there during nearly twenty years. He was frank, bluff, even harsh in his speech and manner, but kind at heart, and it is told of him that once when he discovered a wretched neighbor robbing his corn crib, he moved out of sight that the man might not know he had been caught in the misdeed to which want had driven him.

Thomas Ewing, at one time United States senator from Ohio, and at all times a leading statesman and lawyer, was a citizen of Athens County, where his father settled in 1798. There the boy led the backwoods life, and struggled with all its adversities in his love of books, until he was nineteen. He loved the woods, too, and his boyhood was not unhappy, though his ambition was for the things of the mind. In his reminiscences, he tells of his early privations and of his delight in the first books which came to his hands: the "Vicar of Wakefield," which he learned largely by heart, and the "Aeneid" of Vergil, which he used to read aloud to the farm hands on Sundays, and at such other leisure times as they all had amidst the work of clearing the land. At nineteen, he went to earn some money at the Salines on the Kanawha, and then lavished it upon the luxury of three months' study at Athens. After several years' labor in the salt works, he entered college at Athens, teaching school between terms, and going to Gallipolis to pick up French among the survivors of the disastrous settlement there. Then he turned to the law, and won his way to ease and honor. One of his daughters, as we know, became the wife of General Sherman, whom he had adopted as his son.

Benjamin Lundy, the meek and dauntless Quaker who was called the Father of Abolitionism, lived a long time in Belmont County, at St. Clairsville, where he founded his Union Humane Society, in 1815, and inspired the formation of like societies throughout the country. He was born in New Jersey, and had settled in Wheeling, Virginia, but life there became unendurable to him from the sight of slaves chained and driven in gangs through the streets, on their way to be sold in the Southern markets. In Belmont County, also, the first native Ohio governor, Wilson Shannon, was born.

One of the Ohioans whom history will not forget was Robert Morris, of Clermont County, our United States senator from 1813 till 1839. He was one of the earliest American statesman to own the right of the slave and to defend it. In his last speech he startled the Senate with the prophetic words in which he recognized the danger hanging over the Union, and he said, "That all may be *safe,* I conclude that the Negro will yet be free."

Harrison

Benjamin Harrison, one of the five presidents whom Ohio has given the country within thirty years, was born at North Bend in Hamilton County, where his grandfather General William Henry Harrison lived until chosen President in 1840. He remained in Ohio until he was twenty-one; then he went to Indianapolis, and it was from Indiana that he went to the war, where he achieved rank and distinction by his talent and courage. He is a great lawyer, as well as a soldier and politician, and a speaker of almost unsurpassed gifts.

Chase

Salmon P. Chase, Governor of Ohio and United States senator, Lincoln's first Secretary of the Treasury, and Chief Justice of the Supreme Court of the United States, was an Ohioan by grace of New Hampshire, where he was born, and where he lived till he was a well-grown boy. In 1830, when he was twenty-two years old, he began the practice of law in Cincinnati, and prospered in spite of his bold sympathy with the slave and the friends of the slave. The Kentuckians called him the attorney-general of the Negroes, and the Negroes gave him a silver pitcher, in gratitude for his "public services in behalf of the oppressed." He was first an abolitionist, but later became a leader of the anti-slavery party, and was one of the first and foremost Republicans. As Secretary of the Treasury his mastery in finance was as essential to our success in the war as the statesmanship of Lincoln or the generalship of Grant. He was followed in the office of Chief Justice by another Ohioan of New England birth, who, like Chase, had passed all the years of his public life in our state. Morrison R. Waite, of Toledo, was perhaps even more Ohioan in those traits of plainness and simplicity in greatness which we like to claim for Ohio, only upon sober second thought to acknowledge that they are the distinctive American traits.

An Ohio Secretary of the Treasury assured to the nation the means of meeting the expenses of the Civil War, Ohio generals fought it to a victorious close, and an Ohio Secretary of War knew how to deal best with both the men and the money, so as to turn the struggle from its doubtful course.

Without Edwin M. Stanton neither Chase nor Grant, with Sherman and Sheridan, could have availed. He was born at Steubenville in 1814, of a family of North Carolina Quakers, and as a boy his tastes were as peaceful as those of his ancestors. He had pets of all kinds, and he made collections of birds and insects. He was pretty diligent at school, but his studies there were not of the severer kind. He loved poetry; he founded a circulating library; and both before and after he went to Kenyon College, he was clerk in a bookstore. But deep within this quiet outside was the hot nature which fused the forces of the great war, and shaped them according to his relentless will. He became a successful lawyer, and had been President Buchanan's Attorney-General when Lincoln made him Secretary of War. He left that office worn out with the duties to which he gave mind and body, and died soon after Grant had appointed him, in

1869, to the bench of the Supreme Court. No man in office ever deserved more friends, or made more enemies. He was tender and kindly with the friendless and hapless, but with the strong and the fortunate, when they crossed his mood, he was rude to savagery.

John Sherman

The chief citizen of Richland County is John Sherman, who is also one of the chief citizens of Ohio, and of the United States. He has been in Congress ever since 1855, and ever since 1861 he has been in the Senate, except for the four years when he was Secretary of the Treasury under President Hayes. If any man in our public life during this long period merits more than he the name of statesman, it would be hard to say who he may be. But in his boyhood he gave promise of anything but the sort of career which he has dignified. He had all the impulsiveness of his famous brother, General Sherman, and something more than his turbulence. He himself, with that charming frankness which seems peculiarly a Sherman trait, tells in his autobiography what reckless things he did, even to coming to blows with his teacher; but all this heat seems later to have gone to temper a most manly and courageous character for a career of the greatest public usefulness.

He was born at Lancaster in 1810, and the second President who has called him from the Senate to a seat in his cabinet was born at Niles in Trumbull County, in 1844. William McKinley entered the army as a private in the famous 23d Ohio, when he was only seventeen, and fought through the war. When it ended he had won the rank of brevet major, but he had then his beginning to make in civil life. He studied law, and settled in Canton, where he married, and began to be felt in politics. He was thrice sent to Congress, and then defeated; but in 1896 he was elected the fifth President of the United States from the state of Ohio.

McKinley

It is a long step backward in time, in fact more than a hundred years, before we reach the birthday, in 1794, of Thomas Corwin, one of the most gifted Ohioans who has ever lived.

Corwin

He was born in Kentucky and was brought, a child of four years, by his parents to Ohio, when they settled at Lebanon in Warren County. He grew up in the backwoods, but felt the poetry as well as the poverty of the pioneer days, and it is told that the great orator showed his passion for eloquence at the first school he attended. He excelled in recitations and dialogues; but he was not meant for a scholar by his father and he was soon taken from school, and put to work on the farm. In the War of 1812 he drove a wagon in the supply train for General Harrison's army, and the people liked to call him the Wagoner Boy, when he came forward in politics. A few years later he read law, and with the training which he had given himself at school as well as in the old fashioned debating societies which flourished everywhere in that day, he quickly gained standing at the bar as an advocate. He was all-powerful with juries, and with the people he was always a favorite. Such a man could not long be kept out of public life. He was called to serve seven years in the state legislature and ten in Congress; then he was elected governor. He was so beloved that when he was nominated a second time for the governorship it was taken for granted that he would be elected, but so few of his friends were at the trouble to vote for him that he was, to the profound astonishment of everybody, defeated.

It was a joke which no one could enjoy more than Corwin himself; for he was not only an impassioned orator, but a delightful humorist. He could put a principle or a reason in the form of a jest so that it would go farther than even eloquence could carry it with the whimsical Western people; and perhaps nothing more effective was said against the infamous Black Laws which forbade the testimony of negroes in the courts than Corwin put in the form of self-satire. He was of a very dark complexion, so that he might have been taken for a light mulatto; and he used to say that it was only when a man got to be of about his color that he could be expected to tell the truth.

He was sent to the United States Senate soon after his defeat for the governorship, and it was there that in 1847 he made his great speech against the war with Mexico, as a war of conquest for the spread of slavery. It may be that there are more eloquent passages in English than some of the finest in this speech, where he warned the American people against the doom of unjust ambition, but I do not know them. It was the supreme effort of his life, but it was addressed to a time of unwholesome patriotic frenzy, and Corwin's popularity suffered fatally from it. He never disowned it; he defended and justified it before the people; but he declined from the high stand he had taken as the champion of freedom and justice, and the later years of his political life were marked by rather an anxious conservatism. His final efforts were unavailingly made to stay the course of secession by suggestions of impossible compromise between the North and South. At the close of the war he was stricken with paralysis while visiting as a private citizen the Capitol at Washington, where he had triumphed as representative and senator, and he died almost before the laughter had left the lips of the delighted groups which hung about him. Of all our public men he was most distinctively what is called, for want of some closer term, a man of genius, and he shares with but three or four other Americans the fame of qualities that made men love while they honored and revered him. In the presence of this great soul, so simple, so sweet, so true, so winning, so wise, I think the reader will scarcely care to be reminded that among the notable Ohio men of our day are some of the richest, if not the very richest, American millionaires.

Chapter Twenty-Five
Other Notable Ohioans

TWO names well-known in literature belong to Ashtabula County. Albion W. Tourgee was born there in 1838, and made a wide reputation by his novels, "A Fool's Errand" and "Bricks without Straw," — impassioned and vivid reports of life in the South during the period of reconstruction; and Edith Thomas, who was born in Medina County, made Ashtabula her home till she went to live near New York. While she was still in Ohio, the poems which are full of the love of nature and the sense of immortal things began to win her a fame in which she need envy no others of our time.

One of the earlier Ohioans of note was John Cleves Symmes, of Butler County, who believed that the earth was penetrated at the poles by openings into a habitable region within it. He petitioned Congress for means to explore the Arctic seas and verify his theory; of course he petitioned in vain, but he won world-wide attention and made some converts. He had been a gallant officer of the United States Army, and had fought well in the War of 1812, but he died poor and neglected. He was of New Jersey birth, and of that stanch New Jersey stock which gave character to the whole southwestern part of Ohio.

Another and still more famous theorist, who is not generally known to have been an Ohioan, was Delia Bacon, who first maintained that the plays and poems of Shakespeare were written by Sir Francis Bacon. She was born in Portage County at Tallmadge, where her father was settled as minister.

A sculptor who, if not the greatest American sculptor, has yet achieved in his art the most American things ever done in it, is J. Q. A. Ward, the author of the "Indian Hunter," and many other noble if less native works. He was born at Urbana, in Champaign County, of the old pioneer stock; and in a region remote from artistic influences, he felt the artistic impulse in his boyhood. His earliest attempt was a figure modeled in the wax which one of his sisters used in making wax flowers, and which he clandestinely borrowed. Then he made a bas-relief of the first train of cars he ever saw, but this he did in clay at the village potter's; and he also modeled in clay the head of a negro, well known in the place, which all the neighbors recognized. A few years later he was sent to school in Brooklyn, where he used every day to pass the studio of the sculptor H. K. Browne, and long for some accident that would give him entrance. The chance came at last; he told the sculptor the wish of his heart, and Browne consented to let him try his hand under his eye. From that time the boy's future was assured. The famous sculptor lives absorbed in his work in New York, where his ripe years find him crowned with the honor that will survive him as long as his bronzes and marbles endure.

To Clinton County belongs the name of Addison P. Russell, whose charming books of literary comment have so widely endeared him to book lovers; but whose public services in his own state are scarcely known outside of it among the readers of "Library Notes," or of "A Club of One."

The inventor of the first successful electric light, Charles Francis Brush, was born on his father's farm in Euclid, Cuyahoga County, in 1840, and still pursues in Cleveland the studies which have literally illumined the world. One of the earliest pioneers of science in geology and archaeology, Charles Whittlesey is identified with Cleveland, where the girlhood of the gifted novelist, Constance Fenimore Woolson, was passed. There, too, Charles F. Browne began to make his pseudonym of Artemus Ward known, and helped found the school of American humor. He was born in Maine; but his fun tastes of the West rather than the East.

Edison

Thomas A. Edison, the electrician whose inventions are almost of the quality of miracles and have given him worldwide celebrity, was born in Milan, Erie County, in 1847 of mixed American and Canadian parentage. His early boyhood was passed in Ohio, but he went later to Michigan, where he began his studies in a railroad telegraph office, after serving as a train boy.

Another noted name in science is that of T. G. Wormley, long a citizen of Columbus, though a native of Pennsylvania. He wrote his work on poisons in our capital, where he had studied their effects on animal life, in several thousand cats and dogs, while a professor in Starling Medical College. His microscopical analysis was illustrated by drawings of the poison crystals, made by his wife, who learned the art of steel engraving for the purpose, when it was found that no one else could give the exquisite delicacy and precision of the original designs. Her achievement in this art was hardly less than her husband's in science, and it is a pleasure to record that she was born in Columbus.

To Franklin County also belongs the honor of being the birthplace of the botanist, William S. Sullivant. The American Academy of Arts and Sciences recognized him as the most accomplished student of mosses whom this country has produced.

John S. Rarey

I do not think it at all the least of her honors that Franklin County should be the birthplace of the horse tamer John S. Rarey, for whose celebrity the world was once not too large. He imagined a gentle art of managing horses by study of their nature and character and in Europe, as well as America, he showed how he could subdue the fiercest of them to his will, through his patient kindness. In England the ferocious racing colt Cruiser yielded to Rarey and everywhere the most vicious animals felt his magic. He was the author of a "Treatise on Horse Taming" which had a great vogue in various languages and he achieved a reputation which was by no means mere notoriety.

Coates Kinney of Xenia was not born in Greene County, or even in Ohio; but he came to our state from New York when a boy, he has lived here ever since, and has been shaped by its life. His poem of "Rain on the Roof" is a household word, and it is the poem which will first come into the reader's mind at the mention of his name. But his greatest poem is "Optim and Pessim," which is one of the subtlest and strongest passages of human thought concerning the mystery of the universe; and his next greatest is his "Ode for the Ohio Centennial," delivered at Columbus in 1888. It merits a place with the best that have celebrated, like Lowell's "Commemoration Ode," the achievements of the people.

In Greene County began the long journalistic life of William D. Gallagher, who was born in Philadelphia in 1808, but came while a child to Southern Ohio, and grew up in the impassioned love of that beautiful country. There was not much besides its beauty to endear it to him, for his life was a long struggle there with adverse conditions. But he never lost heart or hope; he failed cheerfully in one literary enterprise after another, and turned from literature to politics until he found the means and the chance to fail again in the field where his heart was always. In Xenia, in Cincinnati, in Columbus, in Louisville, he lived, now here, now there, as his hopes and enterprises called him, and ended at last on a little farm in Kentucky. His poetic vein was genuine; it was sometimes overworked, but at least one poem of entire loveliness was minted from it; and there are few American poems which impart a truer and tenderer feeling for nature than Gallagher's "August," beginning—"Dust on thy summer mantle, dust."

Reid

The life of Whitelaw Reid, who was born near Xenia in 1837, is a romance of success from the beginning, of the kind that seems peculiarly American. His people were Scotch Covenanters, with the stern convictions of that race. It is said that his grandfather first settled in Hamilton County, but rather than run a ferry boat on Sunday, as the deed of his land bound him to do, he sold it and removed to Greene County, where his father was a farmer when the boy Whitelaw was born. He sent his son to school and to college, and then left him to make his own way in the world, which he did by first becoming a country editor, and then going to the war as a newspaper correspondent, and taking part in several battles as an aid-de-camp. He learned to know the war at first hand, and he was well fitted to make his history of "Ohio in the War" the most important of all the state histories. He spent two years in writing this work of truly Ohioan proportions and of unfailing interest, and then he became Horace Greeley's assistant on the *New York Tribune.* It was in the course of nature that after Greeley's death he should become its owner and director, and should take a leading part in national politics. He has been our minister to France, and has acquired great wealth as well as honor; but he has remained affectionately true to the home of his youth, as his care of the old farmstead at Cedarville evinces.

Among the most eminent and useful citizens of the state was Nicholas Longworth, who came from New Jersey to Cincinnati, when just of age, in 1803. He was first to introduce the culture of grapes and the making of wine into Ohio; he planted the Catawba vine on the uplands of Cincinnati, where it flourished till the destruction of the forests changed the climate. He became very rich by his investments in lands, but he never outgrew his sympathy with the poor and struggling, and his hand was open to everyone who could intelligently profit by his help. Many stories are told of his eccentricity. He was so simple in his dress that he was once mistaken for one of his own workmen by a stranger whom he had shown through his grounds, and who gave him a dime; Longworth thanked him and put it in his pocket. For a long time he received the poor every Monday morning at his house, and gave whoever asked a loaf of bread, or a peck of meal, or their worth in money. His charity was of the divine order which does not seek desert in its objects. "I will help the devil's poor," he said, "the miserable drunken dog, whom nobody else will do anything for but despise and kick," and he left the deserving poor to others, knowing that they were sure of friends.

Hiram Powers was the first American sculptor to give us rank in Europe. Longworth, who loved the arts as well as the industries, helped him to go to Florence from Cincinnati, where he had begun by modeling wax figures for a local museum. James H. Beard came from Painesville to Cincinnati, and won there his first success as a portrait painter. He was later to reveal the peculiar satirical gift for expressing human character in animals, for which his brother William H. Beard is perhaps even more famed. Among later artists, either born or bred in Cincinnati, Frank Dengler in sculpture, and Mr. Frank Duvaneck in painting, have shown extraordinary qualities. Dengler died at twenty-four, but not too soon to have given proof of his great talent; Mr. Duvaneck did such things in painting as to attract wide notice in America and Europe, where he headed a revolt of the young painters from the Munich School, and may be said almost to have founded a school of his own. These two young men were of the German stock which flourishes amid the Rhine-like hills of the Ohio; but another gifted Ohioan, who began his art life at Cincinnati, though he was born in Trumbull County, is of that pure American lineage commonest in the Western Reserve. Kenyon Cox, now president of the Art Student's League in New York, is the son of the distinguished statesman and soldier, General J. D. Cox, who was one of the first to enter the army from civil life, and with Garfield and Hayes, to show military qualities second only to those of the West Point men.

Of this class of our generals was Ormsby M. Mitchell, the eminent astronomer in charge of the observatory at Cincinnati, who was among the first to go from that city to the war. He won rank and honor without fighting a battle, by virtue of the same qualities which enabled him to do more than anyone else towards founding a public observatory at Cincinnati before any city in the East had one.

He was of Kentucky birth, and came as a child to Ohio; but William H. Lytle, dear to lovers of poetry as the author of the fine lyric, "Antony and Cleopatra," was born in Cincinnati, of the old Scotch-Irish stock, in 1826. He had everything pleasant in life and he enjoyed his prosperity, but when the war came he met its call halfway. At Chickamauga he fell, pierced by three bullets, in the thick of the fight. As he dropped from his horse into the arms of friends, he smiled his gratitude, and spent his last breath in urging them to save themselves, and leave him to his fate. The poem which begins with the well-known words, "I am dying, Egypt, dying," will keep the name of Lytle in remembrance perhaps longer than all the poems of Phoebe and Alice Cary shall live, such are the caprices of fame; but the verse of these sisters is a part of American literature, as they themselves are a part of its history. They were true poets, and in their work a sense of "The broad horizons of the West" first made itself felt. They left the farm where they were born near College Hill and came to live in Cincinnati after they began to be known in literature, and later they went to dwell among the noises of New York, where they died; but the country, the sweet Miami country, remained a source of their inspiration, and now and again the reader tastes its charm in their verse.

Mrs. Stowe

They were undeniably Ohioan, while Pennsylvania may dispute our right to the fame of Thomas Buchanan Read, though his most famous poem, "Sheridan's Ride," was written and first recited in Cincinnati. We must not more than remind ourselves that Mrs. Harriet Beecher Stowe passed part of her early life in that city, and is known to have gathered much of the suggestion for "Uncle Tom's Cabin" among the Ohio scenes where some of its most vivid events occur.

Kennan

In the county of Huron a man of unquestionable claim to remembrance was born. George Kennan, whose enviable privilege it was to let the light in upon the misery of Siberian exile and to awaken the abhorrence of the world for Russian tyranny was a native of Norwalk, where he grew up a telegraph operator. He worked at night and went to school by day, and when only nineteen, while one of the chief operators in Cincinnati, he applied for leave to join an expedition for laying a cable from Alaska to Siberia by way of Bering Strait. He was asked if he could get ready to start in two weeks, and he answered that he could get ready to start in two hours. He was appointed, and in this way he came to know the horrors which he afterwards studied more fully in a second visit to Siberia. He traveled fifteen hundred miles through that wintry prison of Russia, and saw and heard the sorrowful things which the despotism of the Czar has done to men who dare to love freedom.

His report of these cruelties has at least put their authors to shame before the civilized world, if it has not wrought so great an open change as the work of another Ohio man in dealing with even greater atrocities. It is interesting to note that Januarius A. MacGahan was born in the same county as Philip H. Sheridan, of the same Irish parentage, to the same Catholic religion, and the same early poverty. He saw the light in July, 1844, in a log cabin on his father's little farm among the woods near New Lexington in Perry County. He studied hard at school, and read constantly out of school, when a boy. When a little older, he worked for the neighboring farmers; he hoped to get a school to teach; but he could not get it in his own home, where he was thought too young, and he had to go to Indiana for it. From there he went to St. Louis, where he became a newspaper reporter. In 1868 he sailed for Europe to study French and German, hoping to come home and practice law in that city. But his duty as correspondent took him to the scenes of various European wars, and launched him at last amidst the barbaric outrages of the Turks in Bulgaria. His exposure of their abominable misdeeds in 1876 roused the whole world; the English government officially examined his facts and found them indisputable. The war began between Russia and Turkey, and MacGahan returned to Bulgaria with the victorious Russian troops. There, wherever the people knew him, they hailed him as their savior. He had made their miseries so widely known to mankind as to render it impossible that they should continue. It is not strange that they thronged upon him, and kissed his hands, his boots, his saddle, his horse. In the peace that followed, a whole empire was torn from the bloody hands of the Turks, and four Christian peoples were saved from their savage rule. Bulgaria, Roumania, Roumelia, and Servia now belong to themselves, and all this has come about from the efforts of an unknown young Ohio man, who went abroad to study the languages, and changed the map of Europe. It reads like wild romance, but it is sober history.

Among all these Ohioans of celebrity we must not forget Johnnie Clem, the Drummer Boy of Shiloh. He ran away from his home in Newark, his native city, in 1861, when he was not yet ten years old, and joined the 24th Ohio as drummer; but he was afraid to be seen and sent home by an uncle who was in that regiment, and he cast his lot with the 22d Michigan. He was not only at Shiloh, but the battles of Perryville, Murfreesboro, Chattanooga, Chickamauga, Nashville, and Kenesaw. He was taken prisoner in Georgia, and when his captors stripped him of his clothes he grieved for the loss of nothing except his cap, which had three bullet holes in it. After his release, he came home to get well, and then returned to the army, where General Thomas attached him to his staff. Later he was sent to West Point, where he could not be regularly entered because he was too small; but he made his studies, and Grant commissioned him as lieutenant, and he rose to be captain of infantry. He won the love and respect of all his generals, and while they lived they wrote him letters of affectionate friendship. He was once wounded by a shell, and once he lost his drum by the fragment of a bursting bomb.

J. J. Piatt, who is first among Ohio poets, was born in Indiana; but his boyhood was passed mostly in Ohio, where he grew up on his father's farm, amidst the scenes which he has loved to depict in his verse, until he became a printer's apprentice. Since then he has dwelt in cities, both at home and abroad; but he is always happiest in dealing with the traits and aspects of country life, especially in the earlier times. He was for many years consul at different points in Ireland; and he has found in England even greater recognition for the distinctively mid-western quality of his poems than he has enjoyed among ourselves. So far as he is of Ohio, he is of Logan County, which has been the seat of his family from the settlement of the country; as his name suggests, he is of French descent.

Of Toledo, and therefore of Lucas County, was David R. Locke, who was born in New York state, but lived in Ohio from his fifth year onward. He was a printer and an editor, and after the war, he suddenly won national fame as the author of the Petroleum V. Naseby letters. These were satires of the old proslavery spirit which retarded the reconstruction of the South and harried the freedmen by mobs and lynchings. Their humor gave Locke a place in our literature which no history of it can ignore.

Another literary man who must be taken account of in the summing up of American literature was S. S. Cox, who made himself known early in the fifties when Ohio was far less heard of than now, by his lively book of travels, "A Buckeye Abroad." He was a journalist and a politician; he was three times elected to Congress from Columbus, and when he went to live in New York, he was three times sent to the House of Representatives from that city, where he is commemorated by a statue. He was a native of Muskingum County, and was born in 1824 at Zanesville.

The latest and most brilliant contribution of Ohio to the scholarship of the East is Professor W. M. Sloane, now of Princeton University, but by birth of Jefferson County. He must rank by his "Life of Napoleon" among the American historians of the first class. He is of Scotch Calvinistic ancestry, and the son of a Presbyterian minister.

In this list of Ohioans who have done honor to our state, Mr. James Ford Rhodes happens to be last, though chance might well have placed him among the first. He is the author of "A History of the United States from the Compromise of 1850," which has a peculiar value in the field of American history, and which has given Mr. Rhodes prominent standing, with a constantly growing reputation. He is of the New England race of the Western Reserve; until within a few years his home was in Cleveland, but he now lives in Boston.

Chapter Twenty-Six
Incidents and Characteristics

NEARLY all the Ohio stories since 1812 have been stories of business enterprise and industrial adventure. I dare say that if these could be fully told, we should have tales as exciting, as romantic and pathetic as any I have set down concerning the Indian wars. But such stories are usually forgotten in the material interest of the affairs, and it is only when some tragedy or comedy arising from them finds chance record that we realize how full of human interest they are. The decay of steamboating and the rise of railroading is in itself a romance if it could be rightly seen, and if the facts could be clearly set before us, the story of commercial triumph by a great monopoly would not be less fascinating than that of any war of conquest.

The greatest monopoly of ancient or modern times, the Standard Oil Company, had its rise in Ohio and there is no more impressive chapter in the annals of our country than its history forms. In fact, everything concerning the discovery of the great underground lakes of petroleum and subterranean spaces of natural gas which suddenly enriched certain sections of the state, and then with their exhaustion left them to lapse into ruin, is picturesque and dramatic. Many tales are told of poor farmers who struck oil on their lands and sold them for sums greater than they had ever dreamed of, and then went out into the world to waste their wealth in a few years of wild riot, or sank down and led idle and useless lives in sight of the fields they had once tilled.

Similar stories are told of the regions where natural gas has been found, and some day, when the chronicles of Findlay in Hancock County, are fully written, we shall know all these romantic episodes in their grotesqueness and their pathos. It had been known from the earliest settlement of the country that the natural gas underlay the town and fifty years ago two small wells were sunk. But it was not until after the discovery of the natural gas at Pittsburg that the people of Findlay began to think of turning their treasure to account. Then, in the year 1884, the first great well was bored and sent into the startled air a shaft of flame sixty feet high. Other wells were sunk, and the greatest of all, the famous Karg well, shook its flag of fire against the sky with a roar like that of Niagara and made its voice heard fifteen miles away. It was winter when it was first lighted, but it made summer for two hundred yards around. The snow melted, the grass and wild flowers sprang up and the crickets came and trilled in the grateful warmth. By a sad irony this source of future wealth became the refuge of homeless men and within its genial circuit many tramps slept sweetly, secure from the winter beyond.

Findlay grew from five thousand to fifteen thousand inhabitants in a year. The municipality wisely possessed itself of the most important wells and supplied the gas so cheaply and abundantly to the people that no company could rival it. In June, 1887 it celebrated the anniversary of the first use of the natural gas in the industrial arts and for three days the town was given over to rejoicing in its glory and prosperity. The streets were arched with flame, the great wells flaunted their banners night and day and the gas flared from innumerable pipes and jets through sun and rain in every part of the town.

No such festival has commemorated the introduction of the grape culture in Ohio, though this is one of the most poetic facts of our history. When the changes of climate along the Ohio River rendered it unprofitable in the region of Cincinnati, where the imaginative genius of Longworth had first invented the Catawba wine which the poetic genius of Longfellow celebrated in graceful song, the vine found home and welcome along the shores of Lake Erie. There thousands upon thousands of acres now spread interminable vineyards and the grapes of every American variety purple in autumn to an almost unfailing harvest.

It was at first only a dream when Longworth transplanted the wild vine from the woods and it might well have been scoffed at as akin to dreams of the past which never were realized. One of these was the silk culture, which people believed was to be one of our greatest sources of wealth sixty or seventy years ago, when they planted millions of mulberry trees to nourish the silkworms which died rather than become citizens of Ohio. Another was the culture of the Chinese sorghum cane, which for many years tantalized our farmers with the hopes of native sugar never fulfilled.

Still other kinds of dreams there have been native to our air or naturalized to it. The Leatherwood God was by no means the only religious impostor who has flourished among us. In 1831 Joseph Smith, the first of the Mormon prophets and the founder of Mormonism, came to Portage County with one of his disciples and began to preach. They made so many converts that some shortsighted people of Hiram thought to stop their work by tarring and feathering them. This only drove them from the place, but the next year, they settled in Kirtland, Lake County, where, in 1834, their followers built the first Mormon temple for the worship of God according to the Book of Mormon. It was this sacred book, written on gold plates which Smith, a native of Vermont, pretended to find in a hill near Palmyra, New York, where he was leading an idle and useless life.

His converts at Kirtland increased to three thousand, but they founded a bank as well as a temple, and so got into debt and trouble. Smith left the state to escape the sheriff and went to Missouri where the great mass of the believers joined him, seven hundred leaving Kirtland in one day. Before long the Missourians foolishly began to persecute them and then the Mormons settled at Nauvoo in Illinois where they built their second temple, far more magnificent than the first at Kirtland. But here again their unwise neighbors began to molest them and Joseph Smith and his brother Hiram were thrown into jail. A mob attacked the jail and the Smiths were murdered. The Mormons then abandoned Nauvoo and took their way through the desert to Salt Lake in Utah where they laid the foundations of a great commonwealth. They still own their first temple at Kirtland, however, and it is said to be the hope of one sect among them yet to return and dwell there.

Among the fanaticisms or enthusiasms which flourished among our people, none was more striking than that which moved the Woman's Temperance Crusade in Hillsborough, Highland County, in 1873. Under the influence of a fervent speaker, who told how the women of his native village in New England had joined in beseeching the liquor sellers of the place to give up their traffic, a hundred and fifty ladies of Hillsborough banded together and went about to the different saloons, entreating their owners not to sell strong drink any more. By day and by night, in wet and in cold, through menace and insult, they kept up their effort the whole winter long. Where the dealer was very obstinate, they knelt down at his door and prayed and sang till he yielded. After the crusade ended, the liquor selling began again but though it seemed to have done little good, yet it is said that there has been far less drunkenness in the region than before and public opinion was roused to enforce the laws against liquor selling. Among the crusaders were some of the first ladies of the neighborhood and good women emulated their efforts in several other places.

I am willing to leave the reader with the impression that the people of Ohio are that sort of idealists who have the courage of their dreams. By this courage they have made the best of them come true and it is well for them in their mainly matter-of-fact and practical character that they show themselves at times enthusiasts and even fanatics. It is not ill for them that they should now and then have been mistaken. This has helped to keep them modest in the midst of their prosperity, and their eminence in saving and governing the union of these states. Such as they are, they seem to me, historically, the first of the Americans. The whole country on the eastward characterized them and they, more than the people of any other state, have perpetuated and imparted their character to the whole country on the westward.

Addendum A

Dunmore's War

The British Proclamation of 1763, at the end of the French and Indian war, prohibited colonial expansion and settlement west of the Appalachian Mountains to protect the rights of the Indians occupying the land there. This proclamation did not fare well with the Colonists who claimed that the defeat of the French opened up the territory for settlement by "Right of Conquest" (A principal of law recognized at the time, by all the nations of the world, which gave a conquering nation the right to any territories that they had taken by force of arms.) and that most of the Indians living there had sided with the French and therefore had no rights. This proclamation did not stop some from moving into the restricted territory and hostilities on the frontier heightened.

In 1768 the British Government convinced the Iroquois Six Nation Confederation that they (They Iroquois) were the rightful owners of the lands west of the Appalachians by this same "Right of Conquest" as they had "conquered" the area nearly a century earlier. The Iroquois and the British signed the Treaty of Stanwix and the Iroquois sold the lands to the British Government.

This act infuriated the Indians of the Ohio Country who argued that the Iroquois had no to rights to sell anything. Some Iroquoian Indians sided with the mostly Algonquin speaking Indians of the Ohio Country. These were mostly from the Cayuga and Seneca tribes who formed the western most arm of the Iroquois Confederacy.

One of these was a Cayuga Indian named Logan. Logan had taken this English name in honor of James Logan, a very close friend of his father Shikellamy. Logan and others received permission from the Delaware Indians to settle on the Ohio River near present day Wheeling, West Virginia. Like his father, Logan was a friend to all men, white or red. He was not a major chief of the Mingo Confederation he helped form but he was noted for his wisdom and ability to communicate and resolve problems between the races. He was well respected by both the whites and Indians and his counsel was sought many times to help settle disputes.

On April 30, 1774, a group of Virginia men led by ruffian Daniel Greathouse travelled downriver from near present day Wheeling to the cabin of Joshua Baker, a rum trader who had settled there, across the river from the Mingo Village of Logan. Their intentions were not friendly. Upon arrival Greathouse sent some men across the river to invite Logan and some of his people to come to Baker's cabin for some rum, talk and a little sport. Logan was not at the village. He had gone hunting. Logan's brother, Taylaynee agreed to gather some of his people to cross over the river and join the "party". Among this group were Taylaynee's son Molnah, Logan's wife Mellana, Logan's sister Koonay and her two year old daughter. Koonay was married to John Gibson, an English trader who, at the time, was away on business with the Shawnee. She was pregnant with their second child and very near to giving birth.

Greathouse and his gang enticed the Indians to drink some rum and when they were pretty much intoxicated he proposed a shooting match to see who among them was the best marksman. Of course, he allowed the Indians to take their turn first and as soon as their rifles were emptied, Greathouse and his cutthroats attacked them. They killed, scalped and horribly mutilated their bodies.

One of the most brutal acts perpetrated at that awful scene was when Greathouse tied together the wrists of the pregnant Koonay and hoisted her over a tree limb so her feet were just barely touching the ground. He then took his "hawk", which he always kept razor sharp, and with a huge sweep of his arm slit open her abdomen. He wiped the blood off his hawk and put it back in his belt. Taking his scalping knife, he pulled the baby from her womb and scalped it and threw its lifeless body on the ground. When the firing began, two canoes of Mingo warriors were sent to see what was going on. Greathouse and his gang opened fire on them and drove them back across the river.

The only survivor of this massacre was the two year old daughter of Koonay. She was eventually returned to her father by William Crawford.

Logan upon his return to his village was infuriated, and rightfully so, he gathered warriors from his Mingo Confederation as well as from the Shawnee and Delaware nations and began a series of raids on white settlers in western Pennsylvania. Logan and the Mingo were not the only ones infuriated by this murder. All of the Indians in the Ohio Country clamored for their leaders to strike the war post, take revenge and drive the English back across the Appalachians. Cornstalk of the

Shawnee was one of the few leaders that spoke for reconciliation rather than war but was overruled.

The barbarous, murderous, heinous act perpetrated by the Greathouse gang was the catalyst that started what history has called Dunmore's War and started the chain of events that became a controversy on whether the only major battle fought of that war was not just a colonial war but the first battle of the American Revolution.

These events that culminated in the Battle of Point Pleasant and the signing of a treaty at Camp Charlotte have been a matter of debate for many years and actually began immediately following the battle. Even some of the men who served under Dunmore believed he had deceived them and was actually in collusion with the Shawnee. Some historians believe that the whole situation was planned by Dunmore, a staunch British Loyalist, in an effort to help the Loyalist cause by creating a border war with the Indians and diverting and depleting the Colonist's fighting force in face of the impending Revolution. All this in order to buy time for England to send reinforcements to put it down.

You can read more about the historic events and the controversy surrounding this time in the book "A Point of Controversy" by C. Stephen Badgley. ISBN 978-1456456467.

Addendum B
The Defeat of Harmar and St. Clair

Following the American Revolution, the Indians of the Northwest Territory refused to acknowledge U. S. sovereignty or agree to its claims of ownership of the lands northwest of the Ohio River. In the early and mid 1780's settlers in Kentucky, Virginia, the Ohio country and travelers on the Ohio River suffered around 1500 deaths from Indian attacks carried out by the tribes of Ohio.

In late summer of 1790, General George Washington ordered Brigadier General Josiah Harmar to lead a force of over 1400 men on an expedition against the Indians from Fort Washington (Cincinnati). The Indians attacked them near present day Fort Wayne, Indiana and through the ineptness of General Harmar the force was defeated. They suffered over 120 soldiers killed and over 90 wounded. They were forced to retreat back to Fort Washington. President George Washington then ordered General Arthur St. Clair, who served both as Governor of the Northwest Territory and as a Major General in the Army, to mount a more vigorous effort by the summer of 1791.

Forming the army and obtaining the necessary supplies and equipment was extremely difficult for St. Clair and the summer soon passed. The Army included 600 regulars, 800 six month conscripts and 600 militiamen at its peak but by the time St. Clair was ready to move in late October, there were only around 1450 left as many had deserted. There were also around 200 camp followers made up of wives, children, laundresses and prostitutes who hung around and followed the army.

St. Clair was suffering from gout had difficulty maintaining order and desertions continued to mount. By the first of November, his force had been reduced to a little over 1100 including the camp followers. On November 3rd the force camped on an elevated meadow near present day Fort Recovery, Ohio, close to the headwaters of the Wabash River. They did not construct any defensive works even though Indians had been seen in the forest.

At dawn on November 4th, an Indian force consisting of around 1,000 warriors, led by Little Turtle of the Miami and Blue Jacket of the Shawnee, waited in the woods while the men stacked their weapons and went to their morning meal. They then struck quickly and surprising the Americans, soon overran them.

Little Turtle directed the first attack at the militia, who fled across a stream without their weapons. The regulars immediately broke their musket stacks, formed battle lines and fired a volley into the Indians, forcing them back.

Little Turtle responded by flanking the regulars and closing in on them. Meanwhile, St. Clair's artillery was stationed on a nearby bluff and was wheeling into position when most of the gun crews were killed by Indian marksmen and the survivors were forced to spike their guns and run.

Colonel William Darke ordered his battalion to fix bayonets and charge the main Indian position. Little Turtle's forces gave way and retreated to the woods only to encircle Darke's battalion and destroy it. The bayonet charge was tried numerous times with similar results and the Americans eventually collapsed into disorder. St. Clair had three horses shot out from under him as he tried in vain to rally his men.

After three hours of fighting, St. Clair called together the remaining officers and, faced with total annihilation, decided to attempt one last bayonet charge to get through the Indian line and escape. Supplies and wounded were left in camp. As before, Little Turtle's Army allowed the bayonet charge to pass through but this time the men ran for Fort Jefferson before the Indians could encircle them. The Indians pursued the retreating army for about three miles before they broke off their pursuit and returned to loot the camp. The next day the remnants of St. Clair's force arrived at Fort Jefferson and from there returned to Fort Washington.

The casualty rate at this battle was the highest percentage ever suffered by the United States Army and it included St. Clair's second in command. Of the 52 officers engaged, 39 were killed and 7 wounded. The American casualty rate among the soldiers was 97.4 percent, including 632 of 920 killed and 264 wounded. Nearly all of the 200 camp followers were slaughtered for a total of 832 Americans killed. Approximately one-quarter of the entire U.S. Army had been wiped out. Only 24 of the 920 officers and men engaged came out of it unscathed. Indian casualties were about 60 with at least 21 killed.

Addendum C

Pontiac's Rebellion

In 1763, Ottawa War Chief Pontiac formed a confederation of tribes from the Ohio Country, the Illinois territory and around the Great Lakes regions. Extremely dissatisfied with British policy forced upon them following the defeat of their allies, the French, their goal was to drive all British soldiers and settlers back across the Appalachian Mountains.

In May of 1763, the confederation struck and destroyed eight British forts in the territory northwest of the Ohio River. They went on to raid, kill and capture many settlers in the colonies of Virginia and western Pennsylvania. Many atrocities were committed by both sides during this war. The massacre of women and children, the murders of innocent Native Americans by the Paxton Boys of Pennsylvania and the torturing of British soldiers captured by the Indians are examples of man's inhumanity to man during this bloody era of our nation's history.

It must be noted that during this conflict, the British became the first force in recorded history to employ biological warfare. General Jeffrey Amherst, Commanding General of the British Forces in North America sent a letter to Colonel Henry Bouquet who was preparing to lead an expedition to relieve the forces under siege at Fort Pitt: *"Could it not be contrived to send the small pox among the disaffected tribes of Indians? We must on this occasion use every stratagem in our power to reduce them."*

Bouquet responded with: *"I will try to inoculate the bastards with some blankets that may fall into their hands, and take care not to get the disease myself."*

Amherst's reply: *"You will do well to inoculate the Indians by means of blankets, as well as every other method that can serve to extirpate this execrable race."*

As a result of this, many Indians, men, women and children perished from this horrible disease. Some estimates are in the hundreds of thousands.

The Rebellion officially ended when Pontiac travelled to New York and signed a formal treaty with William Johnson at Fort Ontario on July 25, 1766. England decided it was better to keep the Colonists and the Indians separated. They hurriedly finalized the Royal Proclamation of

1763 which they were working on prior to the rebellion. In an effort to appease the Indians and prevent another uprising, they forbid colonial settlement west of the Allegheny Mountains and reserved the territory for the tribes living there.

This proclamation raised the ire of the Colonists and land speculators because, as they saw it, the Indians had no rights to this land or anything as they had been allies of the defeated French. The land belonged to the Colonists by "Right of Conquest" and should be open to settlement. The proclamation did not deter the expansion of the whites into Indian Territory and conflicts continued. The proclamation became just another factor leading to the Colonist's revolt against the King.

Addendum D

Colonel Crawford's Torture and Death
As witnessed by Dr. John Knight

When we went to the fire the Colonel was stripped naked, ordered to sit down by the fire and then they beat him with sticks and their fists. Presently after, I was treated in the same manner. They then tied a rope to the foot of a post about fifteen feet high, bound the Colonel's hands behind his back and fastened the rope to the ligature between his wrists. The rope was long enough for him to sit down or walk round the post once or twice and return the same way. The Colonel then called to Girty and asked if they intended to burn him?—Girty answered, yes. The Colonel said he would take it all patiently. Upon this Captain Pipe, a Delaware chief, made a speech to the Indians, viz.: about thirty or forty men, sixty or seventy squaws and boys.

When the speech was finished they all yelled a hideous and hearty assent to what had been said. The Indian men then took up their guns and shot powder into the Colonel's body, from his feet as far up as his neck. I think not less than seventy loads were discharged upon his naked body. They then crowded about him, and to the best of my observation, cut off his ears; when the throng had dispersed a little I saw the blood running from both sides of his head in consequence thereof.

The fire was about six or seven yards from the post to which the Colonel was tied; it was made of small hickory poles, burnt quite through in the middle, each end of the poles remaining about six feet in length. Three or four Indians by turns would take up, individually, one of these burning pieces of wood and apply it to his naked body, already burnt black with the powder. These tormentors presented themselves on every side of him with the burning faggots and poles. Some of the squaws took broad boards, upon which they would carry a quantity of burning coals and hot embers and throw on him, so that in a short time he had nothing but coals of fire and hot ashes to walk upon.

In the midst of these extreme tortures, he called to Simon Girty and begged of him to shoot him; but Girty making no answer he called to him again. Girty then, by way of derision, told the Colonel he had no gun, at the same time turning about to an Indian who was behind him, laughed heartily, and by all his gestures seemed delighted at the horrid scene.

Girty then came up to me and bade me prepare for death. He said, however, I was not to die at that place, but to be burnt at the Shawanese towns. He swore by G—d I need not expect to escape death, but should suffer it in all its extremities.

He then observed, that some prisoners had given him to understand, that if our people had had him they would not hurt him; for his part, he said, he did not believe it, but desired to know my opinion of the matter, but being at that time in great anguish and distress for the torments the Colonel was suffering before my eyes, as well as the expectation of undergoing the same fate in two days, I made little or no answer. He expressed a great deal of ill will for Colonel Gibson, and said he was one of his greatest enemies, and more to the same purpose, to all which I paid very little attention.

Colonel Crawford at this period of his sufferings besought the Almighty to have mercy on his soul, spoke very low, and bore his torments with the most manly fortitude. He continued in all the extremities of pain for an hour and three-quarters or two hours longer, as near as I can judge, when at last, being almost exhausted, he lay down on his belly; they then scalped him and repeatedly threw the scalp in my face, telling me "that was my great Captain." An old squaw (whose appearance every way answered the ideas people entertain of the devil,) got a board, took a parcel of coals and ashes and laid them on his back and head, after he had been scalped, he then raised himself upon his feet and began to walk round the post; they next put a burning stick to him as usual, but he seemed more insensible of pain than before.

The Indian fellow who had me in charge, now took me away to Captain Pipe's house, about three-quarters of a mile from the place of the Colonel's execution. I was bound all night, and thus prevented from seeing the last of the horrid spectacle. Next morning, being June 12th, the Indian untied me, painted me black, and we set off for the Shawanese town, which he told me was somewhat less than forty miles from that place. We soon came to the spot where the Colonel had been burnt, as it was partly in our way; I saw his bones lying amongst the remains of the fire, almost burnt to ashes; I suppose after he was dead they had laid his body on the fire.

Index

For more great stories visit the Historical Collection at our website:

www.BadgleyPublishingCompany.com

CPSIA information can be obtained
at www.ICGtesting.com
Printed in the USA
LVHW022324270121
677708LV00038B/770